JAMES

THE FAITH-FUELED COACH

A BIBLE STUDY FOR COACHES WHO
WANT TO PUT THEIR FAITH INTO ACTION

A 12-WEEK STUDY

BRYAN AND JOSHUA MCKENZIE

The Faith-Fueled Coach: James

Cross Training Publishing

www.crosstrainingpublishing.com

(308) 293-3891

Copyright © 2021 by Bryan McKenzie

ISBN: 978-1-938254-10-9

Scripture quotations are from The ESV® Bible (The Holy Bible, English Standard Version®), copyright © 2001 by Crossway, a publishing ministry of Good News Publishers. Used by permission. All rights reserved. The paragraph headings have been changed to provide clarity to the questions and study summaries.

All rights reserved. No part of this book may be reproduced without written permission from the publisher, except by a reviewer who may quote brief passages in a review; nor may any part of this book be reproduced, stored in a retrieval system or transmitted in any form or other without written permission from the publisher.

FOREWORD

I think we would all agree with the brother of Jesus, who wrote the Epistle "James," being only a hearer of God's Word comes up short of also being a doer of the Word. This can lead to deceit and double-mindedness.

James slices through the first century culture with powerful words to the Body of Christ who is experiencing persecution and dispersion. And yet, it rings true through the 22nd century culture as well.

The sports world reflects more than ever what our present-day culture looks like—good, bad, and ugly. Our athletes and coaches get top draw in addressing many personal and social issues as today's media keep "feeding them the ball" when it comes to hearing their perspectives and opinions.

I love that Bryan McKenzie has a uniquely positioned bird's eye view of the sports culture as a former college and professional athlete; former coach; and present-day minister and disciple. Bryan's knowledge of both Scriptures and athletics is evident in this study of the Book of James. But, his understanding of taking the Word of God to the fields, courts, tracks, and playgrounds in the doing of the Word, is not only essential—but exactly what the Book of James is all about.

Ron Brown
Nebraska Football Offense Analyst
Co-founder of Kingdom Sports
www.kingdomsports.online

TABLE OF CONTENTS

INTRODUCTION		7
FORMAT		10
STRATEGY		12
SCOUTING REPORT ON JAMES		14
PREGAME QUESTIONS		16

THE FAITH-FUELED COACH

CHAPTER 1	1:1-12	**TRIALS**	18
CHAPTER 2	1:13-18	**TEMPTATION**	26
CHAPTER 3	1:19-27	**RESPONSE TO THE WORD**	34
CHAPTER 4	2:1-13	**PARTIALITY**	42
CHAPTER 5	2:14-26	**AUTHENTIC FAITH**	52
CHAPTER 6	3:1-12	**THE TONGUE**	60
CHAPTER 7	3:13-18	**WISDOM**	70
CHAPTER 8	4:1-10	**CONFLICT**	80
CHAPTER 9	4:11-17	**PRIDE - PART 1**	90
CHAPTER 10	5:1-6	**PRIDE - PART 2**	100
CHAPTER 11	5:7-12	**PATIENCE IN DIFFICULTY**	110
CHAPTER 12	5:13-20	**PRAYER**	122

INTRODUCTION

Coaches understand the importance of an athlete fueling their bodies to compete at the most optimum level possible. Many athletes talk a good game, but their lack of proper fuel inhibits them from performing at their best. A properly fueled athlete will always come closer to performing at their best over an improperly fueled athlete. That is why coaches educate and encourage their athletes to take in the proper fuel for their bodies.

When it comes to living a life that Glorifies God, what fuels you? Does your faith just talk a good game, or does it fuel you to be a doer of the word and not a hearer only (James 1:22)? In the book of James, God through James encourages, instructs, and illustrates the power of a life that is fueled by an authentic and life-changing faith in Jesus Christ.

Coach, how does your faith fuel you to respond rightly during trials or overcome temptation in your life? How does your faith in Jesus impact how you handle the way the Word of God convicts you of sin? Is your faith on display in the way you treat those who may be hurting on your team? Does your faith empower you to value all your athletes as ones created in the image of God regardless of their performance? Is your faith in Jesus evident in the way you use your words in coaching? How does your faith empower you in dealing with conflict? Does your faith lead to humility in your relationship with God and others? Does your faith express itself through consistent prayer?

Thankfully James addresses all the ways a faith-fueled life impacts each of the questions above. He will encourage and challenge you to grow in your faith in Jesus so God is glorified and others are edified. There are 54 imperatives in the 108 verses in the book of James. This shows that James is urgent to encourage his readers to grow in living a faith-fueled life.

My prayer is that the Lord will use this study of James to inspire and empower you to grow as a faith-fueled coach that brings Him glory and is a blessing to your family, other coaches, and your athletes.

Thank you to my wonderful wife, Jonell, and our six children, who encouraged me during the writing of this study. Thank you for years of inspiring me to live, empowered by God's grace, a faith-fueled life.

Thank you to my parents, Jim and Jennifer McKenzie, who have modeled a faith-fuel life for me to witness. Their love for Jesus, His Word, and people have encouraged me throughout my life.

Thank you to the many coaches who have studied through James with me. Your questions and insights helped me refine much of the way I communicated the truth of James and how it applies to coaches.

Thank you to David and Pam Dupre who graciously proofread and edited the contents of this study. Thank you for your desire to want this study to be clear for the coaches who will use it.

Most of all thank you to the Lord who gave us His inerrant and all sufficient Word to know Him and fuel our faith to Glorify Him.

In Christ,

Bryan McKenzie

DEDICATION

This book is dedicated to all the coaches who have consistently imparted spiritual wisdom to their athletes. Thank you for having biblical discernment and passing it down to the next generation. Your fruit is evident in the lives that are changed. Your reward awaits you in heaven.

FORMAT

The format for this manual is pretty simple.
These are the component parts of each chapter:

CHAPTER TITLE

Summarizes the key concept in one word or phrase.

STUDY STARTER

Helps you understand the importance and relevance of the spiritual truths you're about to study.

STUDY PASSAGE

Gives you the designated biblical text to read and study for the chapter.

STUDY HELP

Provides insight into the meaning of words, interpretation of statements, and explanation of concepts.

STUDY QUESTIONS

Asks questions about the passage you must investigate and answer.

STUDY SUMMARY

Condenses the passage into one singular statement so you can understand the "big idea" of the text.

COACHING CONNECTION

Takes the Study Summary and transfers it to the world of coaching so you can clearly see the Spirit-intended applications of the Word of God on the life of the Christian coach.

KEYS TO WINNING

Guides you to meditate on the spiritual truths in the text and how they should shape your own heart and life as a coach. Each key has a video guide found at www.kingdomsports.online.

GAME CHANGER

Points you to the person and work of Jesus Christ to help you be a faith-fueld coach through the power of the Gospel.

ONE BIG THING

Asks you to consider the most significant lesson you should take with you from the chapter.

IMPACT PRAYER

Motivates you to seek the Lord's help in applying the truths you have learned in each study.

STRATEGY

The strategy for this manual is also quite simple. This is our recommendation:

Recruit a group of coaches to walk through the study with you. These coaches do not have to be Christians to join the study. As a matter of fact, we encourage you to reach out to any and all coaches you think would consider participating.

Secure a copy of this training manual for every coach who participates in the study. You can order more copies at www.crosstrainingpublishing.com

Appoint a leader for the weekly group study. This leader can be a fellow coach, former coach, spiritual leader, or pastor. The key criteria are that this person is a Christian who understands coaches, pursues Christ, and is willing to put in a little extra work to make the group study a powerful time in the Word of God. The group leader has the liberty to elaborate on the text and press into areas that are not necessarily covered in each lesson. This manual is merely a guide. There is freedom to take the study deeper and wider for more growth.

Schedule a weekly meeting day and time for 10-12 weeks. Allocate 45 to 60 minutes for the group study. Put the dates and times in your calendar and consider them high priority.

Invest 30-60 minutes on your own prior to the study familiarizing yourself with the study passage, reading it, answering the study questions, and considering the Study Summary, Coaching Connection, and Keys to Winning. Go to the group study ready to participate, ask questions, provide insight, seek help, and sharpen your fellow coaches in their pursuit of Christ.

Encourage one another throughout the week with the truths you are learning. As iron sharpens iron, so one coach will sharpen another.

Trust God to do a powerful work in your heart and life. The Word of God is living and active, sharper than a two-edged sword. It pierces to the division of soul and spirit, joints and marrow, and discerns the thoughts and intentions of the heart. It will do heart surgery on you if you will surrender yourself to it. So give yourself to this study and watch God work powerfully in and through you.

Read the Scouting Report prior to each study. Just as you try to know as much as you can about your opponent before you play them, you need to know as much as you can about the context of James before you study it.

Don't worry if you can't find another coach to study with you. The best way to profit from this study is with a group of other coaches, but you can certainly do it on your own. If you're a Christian, you have the Spirit of Christ living in you. He will give you illumination along the way. So don't let your isolation from other like-minded coaches discourage you. We encourage you to ask your local pastor, FCA staff, or church leader to walk through it with you. Anyone who loves the Lord and wants to grow into greater maturity could be a great study partner.

SCOUTING REPORT
ON JAMES

SCOUTING REPORT

This letter was written by James in approximately 46-49 A.D. to a group of Jewish followers of Jesus. These Christians, along with many others, had been dispersed outside of Jerusalem because of the persecution of Herod as recorded in Acts 12. These people were outcasts, persecuted, and exploited by the rich and yet they played favorites among each other. They had problems from within their group and problems from outside their group. These Christians were immature in their faith and needed instruction on how they could mature. It seems that many of them had over-reacted to their former life of legalism, in which abiding by rules and regulations made them right with God. Therefore, they believed that knowledge of the truth was sufficient without putting truth into practice. This kind of thinking was wrong and needed to be corrected.

Therefore, James comes along to correct their thinking and help them grow. He wants them to see that faith in Jesus as Lord and Savior fuels every part of their life. He seeks to show them that their actions and reactions are to be evidence of the maturity of their faith in Jesus. In order for them to reach the fallen world around them, their faith needed to be living, growing, productive and evident.

Coach, like these early Christians to whom James writes, you too are called to reach your team with the Gospel of Jesus. In order to most effectively reach them your faith must be living, growing, productive and evident. Your faith must fuel your life. As you study the letter of James over the next 12 weeks allow it to grow your faith in Jesus so that you can more effectively reach your team with the Gospel.

Coach, before you begin this study, ask the Lord to help you learn the truth of His Word through James. Then ask the Lord to help you, by His grace, put these truths into practice so your words and walk will be a testimony to the Gospel.

PREGAME QUESTIONS

1. On a scale a scale of 1 to 10, how would you rate your response to trials in your life?

   1   2   3   4   5   6   7   8   9   10

         Poor   Fair   Good

2. Why did you give yourself the above rating?

   _____
   _____
   _____
   _____

3. How does your faith in Jesus as Lord and Savior show up in your daily interactions with your athletes?

   _____
   _____
   _____
   _____

4. How would you want your athletes to respond to the following question—"What did you learn from your coach in the area of how he/she responded to trials?"

   _____
   _____
   _____
   _____

5. The title of this study is "The Faith-Fueled Coach" because a life fueled by faith in Jesus should be the reality of every Christian coach. If you have truly placed your faith in Jesus as your Savior and Lord, then that faith should fuel your life in the things you do and say.

I challenge you to write out a simple prayer asking God to fuel you in such a way that your faith is evident in all you say and do.

_____
_____
_____

6. If possible, choose another coach to be your partner in this study for mutual encouragement, accountability, and prayer. You can hold one another accountable to do the pre-work, thoughtfully answer the questions, and implement the keys to winning in your coaching. Write his/her name down here and make a weekly communication plan:

_____
_____
_____
_____

CHAPTER ONE
THE FAITH-FUELED COACH
TRIALS

JAMES 1:1-12

STUDY STARTER

As a coach you have no doubt experienced your share of trials. Whether it be difficulty at home, relationships with others on your staff, poor choices by athletes, lack of support from administration, the death of someone in or close to your program, or heart-breaking losses on the field; trials hurt and can often derail progress in your life and coaching career. How you respond to trials in your life will greatly impact you and others around you. Understanding the purpose of trials will enable you to properly respond to them.

STUDY PASSAGE

[1] James, a servant of God and of the Lord Jesus Christ,
To the twelve tribes in the Dispersion: Greetings. [2] Count it all joy, my brothers, when you meet trials of various kinds, [3] for you know that the testing of your faith produces steadfastness. [4] And let steadfastness have its full effect, that you may be perfect and complete, lacking in nothing. [5] If any of you lacks wisdom, let him ask God, who gives generously to all without reproach, and it will be given him. [6] But let him ask in faith, with no doubting, for the one who doubts is like a wave of the sea that is driven and tossed by the wind. [7] For that person must not suppose that he will receive anything from the Lord; [8] he is a double-minded man, unstable in all his ways.
[9] Let the lowly brother boast in his exaltation, [10] and the rich in his humiliation, because like a flower of the grass he will pass away. [11] For the sun rises with its scorching heat and withers the grass; its flower falls, and its beauty perishes. So also will the rich man fade away in the midst of his pursuits. [12] Blessed is the man who remains steadfast under trial, for when he has stood the test he will receive the crown of life, which God has promised to those who love him.

STUDY HELP

- **v. 1 – "servant"** = *a person who is in a permanent relationship of servanthood to another.*
- **v. 1 – "twelve tribes in the Dispersion"** = *Jewish believers living outside of Jerusalem who were dispersed or scattered there because of the persecution of Herod Agrippa as recorded in Acts 12.*
- **v. 2 – "joy"** = *constant delight of the soul based not on favorable circumstances but on a faithful Savior*
- **v. 2 – "meet"** = *(encounter) this word has the idea of being surrounded as if there is no way to escape trials.*
- **v. 2 – "trials"** = *testing from difficulties leading to a desired end*
- **v. 3 – "steadfastness"** = *to remain under a heavy load and resolutely staying there*
- **v. 5 – "wisdom"** = *the practical application of knowledge*
- **v. 5 – "without reproach"** = *does not rebuke those who ask for knowledge*
- **v. 8 – "double-minded"** = *double-souled; trying to go two ways at once*
- **v. 9 – "lowly"** = *poor*
- **v. 9 – "boast"** = *pride or exaltation in something*
- **v. 12 – "stood the test"** = *this phrase was used for the testing of coins and metals to determine their genuineness*

STUDY QUESTIONS

1. How does James refer to himself in verse 1? What does this say about his attitude as a leader as he approaches those who are struggling and most likely not responding well to their struggles?

_____
_____
_____

2. What is the proper response James calls for someone experiencing a trial (v. 2)?

_____
_____
_____

3. What is the purpose of trials presented by James in verses 3 and 4? How would this help you respond appropriately to trials?

_____
_____
_____

4. When you are struggling with understanding the purpose of trials and therefore responding in a wrong way, what does James exhort you to do (vv. 5-8)?

_____
_____
_____

5. Is there a difference of how a poor person and a rich person should relate to their trials (vv. 9-12)? If so, what is it?

_____
_____
_____

6. What is required to receive the crown of life (v. 12)?

_____
_____
_____

STUDY SUMMARY

God wants to use trials in your life to make you more like Jesus and to grow your faith in Him.

COACHING CONNECTION

Coach, God wants you to respond properly to trials, so you can lead your team in learning how to grow from trials and become more like Jesus.

KEYS TO WINNING

▶ **VIDEO GUIDE AT KINGDOMSPORTS.ONLINE**

▶ EXERCISE THE PROPER RESPONSE

James exhorts believers experiencing trials to make a deliberate decision to embrace their God-given trials with an attitude of joy. In fact, James assumes that trials are part of the life of everyone who knows Jesus. Whenever the trials come and in whatever form they come in, we are to respond with an attitude of joy while trusting the Lord as we walk through them.

- How do you normally respond to trials in your coaching? Do you respond with anger, bitterness, giving up, complaining, fear, denial, etc…?

- What is one example of when you were tested as a coach and you responded in the wrong way? How did that impact your team?

- What is one example of when you or a coach you know responded in a positive way to trials? How did that impact your team?

_____
_____
_____
_____
_____

▶ UNDERSTAND THE PURPOSE

No doubt even if we are committed to properly responding to trials with an attitude of joy, it is not easy to do. James understands this, therefore in verses 3-4 he explains the purpose of trials. The purpose of the trials God brings into our lives is to grow our faith in Him and to make us more like Jesus. When we understand God's purpose in trials it helps us to respond properly when they come.

- How have you seen God grow your faith and make you more like Jesus through trials you have experienced as a coach?

_____
_____
_____

▶ EXERCISE PRAYER

The call to respond with an attitude of joy in the midst of trials is challenging. In fact, it almost seems irrational. Therefore, we need wisdom to see trials from God's perspective and allow HIM to mature us in and through them. James exhorts us to ask our generous God for wisdom to understand trials from His perspective and trust that He will supply the wisdom we need.

- In what trial do you currently find yourself or what trial have your recently endured? Take time to write out a prayer asking God to give you wisdom to see the trial from His perspective and show you how He is using it to grow your faith.

▶ **RECEIVE THE PRIZE**

Regardless of our position in life or circumstances (rich or poor) we are a called to respond properly to trials and remain steadfast under them for the purpose of spiritual growth. When we do what James says we receive the prize of the crown of life. In other words, we are blessed with an ever-growing relationship with God as He conforms us more and more into the image of Jesus. Our steadfastness in trials is an ongoing confirmation of our living faith in Jesus.

- Coach, in what areas are you experiencing the prize of seeing God grow your living faith through trials?
- Take a moment to give Him thanks for how He is using trials to grow you and make you more like Jesus.

GAME CHANGER

The Lord Jesus is familiar with trials. Scripture tells us that He was tempted in all ways just as we are (Hebrews 4:15). But what separates His trials from ours is that He never sinned in the midst of His trials. He suffered, but He never gave in. He faced hardship, but

He never gave up. Because He faced trials and suffered hardship on a level that you and I will never know, we can run to Him with our trials. He knows. He cares. He listens. He responds. So whatever trial you are facing today, take it to Jesus.

ONE BIG THING

What is the most significant lesson for you to take from this chapter?

_____
_____
_____
_____
_____
_____
_____
_____
_____

IMPACT PRAYER

Father help me have the proper response to trials in my life and in my sport. Remind me that you are using trials to produce steadfastness and make me more like Jesus. Generously grant me the wisdom you promise, so that I see the trial from your perspective. Empower me to be an example to my athletes and fellow coaches of how to respond to trials in a way that honors You. In Jesus' name I pray, Amen.

✦ ✦ ✦
CHAPTER TWO
THE FAITH-FUELED COACH
TEMPTATION

JAMES 1:13-18

STUDY STARTER

As a coach you have no doubt faced all kinds of temptation. The temptations to coach for popularity, prestige or a new position are always present in our sports crazed culture. The temptation to use fear as a motivator is real, as is the temptation to give up on a player who continually gives into temptation in his own life. There is also the ever-present temptation to neglect your responsibilities at home, because you think that an extra hour in the office is going to make or break you when it comes to winning a championship. Giving into these temptations and others like them is sin and dishonoring to the Lord and HIS call on your life. Whatever your temptations are, they are serious and must be dealt with in a way that honors the Lord.

STUDY PASSAGE

[13] Let no one say when he is tempted, "I am being tempted by God," for God cannot be tempted with evil, and he himself tempts no one. [14] But each person is tempted when he is lured and enticed by his own desire. [15] Then desire when it has conceived gives birth to sin, and sin when it is fully grown brings forth death. [16] Do not be deceived, my beloved brothers. [17] Every good gift and every perfect gift is from above, coming down from the Father of lights, with whom there is no variation or shadow due to change. [18] Of his own will he brought us forth by the word of truth, that we should be a kind of firstfruits of his creatures.

STUDY HELP

- *v. 13 – "tempted"* = testing that has as its desired end evil.
- *v. 14 – "lured"* = when a fish is lured away from its safe place by something attractive.
- *v. 14 – "enticed"* = a fish being caught by bait (hooked).
- *v. 14 – "desire"* = a passionate longing, can either be positive or negative.
- *v. 17 – "perfect"* = complete or sufficient; lacking nothing to meet the need

STUDY QUESTIONS

1. What does James say in regard to God and His relationship with temptation (v. 13)?

___

2. Who does James say is responsible for temptation and the response to temptation (v. 14)? How can this help you as a leader as you train your athletes to take responsibility for their actions?

___

3. What does James teach in regard to the progression of temptation in verse 14-15? How does this help you in your fight against temptation?

___

4. How does James describe God's character in verse 17?

___

5. What is the greatest gift God has given us according to verse 18? What great thing has God done for us? (Also see Ephesians 2:8-9)

_____
_____
_____

6. What is the word of truth (v.18) and how can it be used to fight temptation in your life as a coach?

_____
_____
_____

STUDY SUMMARY

God wants us to acknowledge the source of temptation, understand the sequence of temptation and rely on His solution to overcome temptation.

COACHING CONNECTION

Coach, God provides you a solution: New life though His Word that empowers you to overcome the temptation in your life and display your living faith in Him.

KEYS TO WINNING

▶ **VIDEO GUIDE AT KINGDOMSPORTS.ONLINE**

▶ ACKNOWLEDGE THE SOURCE

What is the source of our temptation? Who is to blame for the temptation in our lives? The world we live in encourages us to pass the blame for giving into temptation and sin to someone or something else. This is not the answer God through James gives us. The first thing James does in pointing to the source of our temptation is to emphatically state that God is NOT the source of temptation (v. 13). The second thing James does in pointing to the source of our temptation is to emphatically state who is the source of temptation. Who is to blame for our temptation and sin? James emphatically says, we are (v. 14). Our temptations come from the unredeemed part of us (referred to as the flesh in the Bible).

- Coach, when you are tempted and give into the temptation, who do you blame? Do you blame God, circumstances, others, your past, etc.?

- How can you keep from shifting blame to others when you do sin as a coach, so that your faith can still be on display?

_____
_____
_____
_____
_____

▶ UNDERSTAND THE SEQUENCE

Knowing and acknowledging the source of our temptations is the first key to overcoming them. We also need to understand the sequence or progression in which temptation comes. James clearly points to this sequence of temptation beginning with desire (v. 14). Desire leads to deception (lured and enticed – v. 14) … deception leads to disobedience (gives birth to sin – v. 15) … and disobedience leads to death (v.15). We must learn to recognize this sequence to begin to battle the temptation in our lives.

- Coach, name a time when you gave into temptation? What led up to your giving into that temptation?
- What can you learn from James that would keep you from giving into a similar temptation in the future?
- How can your battle with temptation in your own life be used as an example for your team?

_____
_____
_____
_____
_____
_____
_____

▶ RELY ON THE SOLUTION

Part of the Solution for Temptation in your life begins with acknowledging the source (you) and understanding the sequence (Desire, Deception, Disobedience, Death) of temptation. However, the solution to temptation does not end there. We must understand that the solution to temptation is found not in us, but in God. We must rely on Him to overcome temptation. James points to the fact that God is the giver of all good gifts (v. 17) and His giving nature never changes (v. 17). His greatest gift is that he gave us new birth (brought us forth – v. 18) and did so through the word of truth (v. 18). Not only does his gift of new birth rescue us from the penalty of sin but it also daily rescues us from the power of sin by enabling us to resist temptation through the word of truth.

- Coach, when you are tempted, how do you resist the temptation? Do you rely on your own strength or God's strength in you? What are you doing daily to allow God to be the solution to your temptation?

- Name the biggest temptation in your life currently. What lie is that temptation based upon? What truth from God's Word combats that lie? Ask God to empower you to put that truth into practice.

_____
_____
_____
_____

GAME CHANGER

The Lord Jesus is not only familiar with trials, He is also familiar with temptation. In Matthew 4 Jesus was tempted by the devil. The devil tempted Him in the areas of "the lust of the flesh, the lust of the eyes and the boastful pride of life (1 John 2:16)." Each time Jesus was tempted by the devil, He refuted his lies by pointing to the truth of God's Word found in Scripture.

Whatever your temptation is, know God is faithful to empower you to stand on the truth of His Word and resist the temptation.

"No temptation has overtaken you that is not common to man. God is faithful, and he will not let you be tempted beyond your ability, but with the temptation he will also provide the way of escape, that you may be able to endure it." – 1 Corinthians 10:13

ONE BIG THING

What is the most significant lesson for you to take from this chapter?

_____
_____
_____
_____
_____

IMPACT PRAYER

Father help me be quick to acknowledge the source of my temptation is me. Give me eyes to see the areas I am tempted in the most. Thank You for being the giver of all good gifts, especially for giving me new life in Christ. Thank You that in my new life in Christ You have also given me the power to resist temptation. Empower me to daily seek You through your Word and prayer in order to grow me in the ability to use Your power to resist temptation. As You empower me, may You use me to be an example to my athletes and fellow coaches of how to overcome temptation so that You are glorified. In Jesus' name I pray, Amen.

CHAPTER THREE
THE FAITH-FUELED COACH
RESPONSE TO THE WORD

JAMES 1:19-27

STUDY STARTER

Every coach enjoys athletes who are coachable. Coachable athletes listen, believe and put into practice the instruction of their coach. In an even greater way, when we, as followers of Christ, enthusiastically embrace the instruction of the Lord, it leads to peace, enjoyment, victory and hope in our lives. In the midst of your trials (vv. 1-12) and temptations (vv. 13-18), how do you respond to God's coaching of you through His Word, the Bible? Do you respond with anger at God's Word, or refuse to look to God's Word, or refuse to obey God's Word, or even take God's Word out of context to justify your sin in the midst of a temptation? How we respond to God's Word in the midst of our trials and temptations is critical in the process of progressively growing in Christ.

STUDY PASSAGE

[19] Know this, my beloved brothers: let every person be quick to hear, slow to speak, slow to anger; [20] for the anger of man does not produce the righteousness of God. [21] Therefore put away all filthiness and rampant wickedness and receive with meekness the implanted word, which is able to save your souls. [22] But be doers of the word, and not hearers only, deceiving yourselves. [23] For if anyone is a hearer of the word and not a doer, he is like a man who looks intently at his natural face in a mirror. [24] For he looks at himself and goes away and at once forgets what he was like. [25] But the one who looks into the perfect law, the law of liberty, and perseveres, being no hearer who forgets but a doer who acts, he will be blessed in his doing. [26] If anyone thinks he is religious and does not bridle his tongue but deceives his heart, this person's religion is worthless. [27] Religion that is pure and undefiled before God the Father is this: to visit orphans and widows in their affliction, and to keep oneself unstained from the world.

STUDY HELP

- *v. 19 - "quick"* = *eager and attentive.*
- *v. 19 - "slow"* = *show restraint.*
- *v. 19 - "anger"* = *a strong, deliberate and persistent feeling of indignation.*
- *v. 20 - "righteousness"* = *the right conduct God prescribes.*
- *v. 21 - "put away"* = *throw off.*
- *v. 21 - "receive"* = *to embrace or grasp.*
- *v. 21 - "meekness"*= *humility.*
- *v. 21 - "save"* = *rescue.*
- *v. 22 - "hearers"* = *a person who audits a class who has no intention to put anything into practice.*
- *v. 22 - "deceiving"* = *to reason falsely.*
- *v. 25 - "looks into"* = *examine closely.*
- *v. 25 - "perseveres"* = *to remain or continue in.*
- *v. 26 - "bridle"* = *the headgear with which a horse is controlled.*
- *v. 27 - "visit"* = *caring for others.*

STUDY QUESTIONS

1. What word found in verses 21, 22 and 23 ties this section of Scripture to verse 18?

_____
_____
_____

2. What does James say is the first way in which we are to respond to His Word (v. 19)? How does this help you as a coach as you train your athletes to be good listeners to your instruction of them?

_____
_____
_____

3. What do we need to do before we can receive God's Word (v. 21)? How does this impact the way you train your athletes to be ready to receive your instruction on and off the field?

_____
_____
_____

4. What is the attitude by which we are to receive God's Word (v. 21)? Coach, how can your humility toward God's Word be modeled to your athletes?

_____
_____
_____

5. What does James say about those who only hear God's Word and not do God's Word (vv. 22-24)?

_____
_____
_____

6. What is the result when we put God's Word into practice (v. 25-27)? How can the doing of God's Word in your life be an example to your athletes of the importance of putting into practice the instruction you give them?

_____
_____
_____

STUDY SUMMARY

God wants us to respond to His Word by hearing, receiving and doing it.

COACHING CONNECTION

Coach, God provides us His Word to put into practice so that we may be delivered from the destructive consequences of a wrong attitude in the trials and temptations we face as a coach.

KEYS TO WINNING

▶ VIDEO GUIDE AT KINGDOMSPORTS.ONLINE

▶ HEAR GOD'S WORD

God through James instructs us to respond rightly to His Word, first by being hearers of His Word. The first thing we need to do in order to be hearers of the Word is to have a heart attitude that is eager and attentive to the Word of God (be quick to hear – v. 19) in the midst of our trials and temptations. The second step in being hearers of the Word is to restrain ourselves from speaking and instead listen and think deeply (be slow to speak – v. 19) about how it applies to our situation. When we do these things, it enhances our ability to hear HIS clear instruction on how to Honor HIM (righteousness of God – v. 20) in the midst of our trial or temptation.

- Coach, what do you need to do in order to have a heart attitude that is eager and attentive to the Word of God?

- When you read God's word or hear it taught by others, do you take the time to think about it deeply and the implications it has on your life? Think of an example when you took the time to think deeply about God's word in a certain area and then applied its truth to your life. What was the impact?

_____
_____
_____
_____

▶ RECEIVE GOD'S WORD

Not only are we to respond to God's Word by being hearers, but we are to respond to His Word by being receivers. James instructs us to eagerly embrace (receive – v. 21) and apply God's Word that was "implanted" when God gave us new birth (v. 18). We are to do this with an attitude that is willing to submit to God's Word (meekness – v. 21). However, before we can properly receive His Word we must first put away (v. 21) every aspect of sin in our life. Our motivation to be good receivers of God's Word is that it results in us being rescued (saved – v. 21) from the consequences of wrong attitudes in trials and wrong actions in temptations.

- Coach, is there a sin with which you need to make a clean break in order to be prepared to receive God's Word? If so, confess it to God, thank him for the forgiveness you have in Christ and ask him for the power to forsake it.

- How can forsaking sin in your life be used to train your athletes to forsake those things in their own life that hinder their ability to be all God designed them to be?

_____
_____
_____
_____

▶ DO GOD'S WORD

After we hear and receive God's Word, He then wants us to put His word into action (be doers – v. 22). James says that not putting God's Word into action in our lives is as ridiculous as someone who after looking in a mirror and seeing something needs to change, does nothing (vv. 23-24). Yet, those who seriously consider God's Word (the Gospel that brings freedom) and put it into practice, are blessed (v. 25). James then gives 3 ways we can specifically put God's Word into action. He exhorts us, by God's grace, to have a controlled tongue (v. 26), a compassionate heart (orphans and widows– v. 27) and a clean life (unstained – v. 27).

- Name a situation as a coach where you have put God's Word into practice and experienced His blessing? How did it impact your athletes?

- Are there athletes you coach who are in situations that need Christ-like compassion? If so, how can He use you to bring that compassion in their lives?

_____
_____
_____
_____
_____

GAME CHANGER

It is so important for us to know that the **doing** of God's Word is never to earn God's favor but should always flow from the position of favor we already have with God through faith in Jesus. We were saved to do good works, not by good works.

"For by grace you have been saved through faith. And this is not your own doing; it is the gift of God, not a result of works, so that no one may boast. For we are his workmanship, created in Christ Jesus for good works, which God prepared beforehand, that we should walk in them." – Ephesians 2:8-10

ONE BIG THING

What is the most significant lesson for you to take with you from this chapter?

_____
_____
_____
_____
_____
_____
_____

IMPACT PRAYER

Father when presented with your Word, empower me to be eager and attentive to Your Word in the midst of trials and temptations. Convict me of sin that I need to put out of my life, so I can embrace Your Word and be rescued from the consequences of a wrong attitude in trials and wrong actions in temptation. Empower me, by Your grace, to put Your Word into practice by having a controlled tongue, a compassionate heart and a clean life. May this all be done for Your Glory. In Jesus' name I pray, Amen.

CHAPTER FOUR
THE FAITH-FUELED COACH
PARTIALITY

JAMES 2:1-13

STUDY STARTER

As a coach, have you ever shown favoritism to an athlete based on their athletic ability? Have you ever treated an athlete better or worse based on their appearance? Have you ever been partial toward an athlete based on their socio-economic status? All of us who have coached can most likely answer "YES" to at least one of these questions. Is this the way a coach, forgiven by the grace of God in Christ, should treat the athletes entrusted to them? We all know the answer to this question is – "NO." God through James is going to address the sin of partiality in the first half of chapter two and give us hope that as a faith-fueled coach, we can overcome it by His grace in us.

STUDY PASSAGE

¹My brothers, show no partiality as you hold the faith in our Lord Jesus Christ, the Lord of glory. ² For if a man wearing a gold ring and fine clothing comes into your assembly, and a poor man in shabby clothing also comes in, ³ and if you pay attention to the one who wears the fine clothing and say, "You sit here in a good place," while you say to the poor man, "You stand over there," or, "Sit down at my feet," ⁴ have you not then made distinctions among yourselves and become judges with evil thoughts? ⁵ Listen, my beloved brothers, has not God chosen those who are poor in the world to be rich in faith and heirs of the kingdom, which he has promised to those who love him? ⁶ But you have dishonored the poor man. Are not the rich the ones who oppress you, and the ones who drag you into court? ⁷ Are they not the ones who blaspheme the honorable name by which you were called? ⁸ If you really fulfill the royal law according to the Scripture, "You shall love your neighbor as yourself," you are doing well. ⁹ But if you show partiality, you are committing sin and are convicted by the law as transgressors. ¹⁰ For whoever keeps the whole law but fails in one point has become guilty of all of it. ¹¹ For he who said, "Do not commit adultery," also said, "Do not murder." If you do not commit adultery but do murder, you have become a transgressor of the law. ¹² So speak and so act as those who are to be judged under the law of liberty. ¹³ For judgment is without mercy to one who has shown no mercy. Mercy triumphs over judgment.

STUDY HELP

- **v. 1 – "partiality"** = prejudice leading to discrimination based on the outward appearance or status of someone.

- **v. 2 – "assembly"** = a public worship gathering.

- **v. 2 – "gold ring"** = literally – gold-fingered indicating multiple rings.

- **v. 2 – "fine clothing"** = bright or shining.

- **v. 2 – "poor"** = one who cowers because they are destitute of wealth, position, honor.

- **v. 3 – "pay attention"** = look upon with favor.

- **v. 4 – "evil thoughts"** = vicious and destructive intentions.

- **v. 6 – "oppress"** = to exploit; a person in authority exercising their power over those under their control in a hurtful way.

- **v. 8 – "royal law"** = summarizes the entire law of God as explained and fulfilled in King Jesus.

- **v. 9 – "transgressors"** = those who pass over a forbidden boundary.

- **v. 12 – "law of liberty"** = law that brings freedom; Gospel.

STUDY QUESTIONS

1. According to verse 1, what is forbidden for those who have faith in the Lord Jesus Christ? Why?

_____

_____

_____

2. What does James say we have done when we show partiality based on person's outward appearance or status (v. 4)? What are you communicating to your athletes when you are showing partiality as illustrated in verses 2-4?

_____
_____
_____

3. According to verses 5-7, how does God's treatment of the poor differ from the treatment by some of Jesus' followers?

_____
_____
_____

4. According to verse 8 what is an indication that our life is being fueled by our faith in Jesus? In what ways would your athletes say you are loving them as yourself?

_____
_____
_____

5. In verses 9-11, to what sins does James equate partiality? How does this emphasize the seriousness of the sin of partiality? Do you consistently deal with partiality on your team like you do other sins? How?

_____
_____
_____

6. According to verses 12-13 what motivation does James give to deter showing partiality?

_____
_____
_____

STUDY SUMMARY

God desires us to value all people and not to show partiality towards anyone.

COACHING CONNECTION

Coach, God fuels our faith by His grace in order that we may overcome the sin of partiality for His glory.

KEYS TO WINNING

▶ **VIDEO GUIDE AT KINGDOMSPORTS.ONLINE**

▶ OBEY THE IMPERATIVE AGAINST PARTIALITY

When it comes to showing partiality, God through James commands us to never to show partiality (v. 1). In other words, we should never treat people differently based on their appearance, athletic ability, economic status, etc. (v. 1). James gives further weight to his imperative with the phrase: "as you hold the faith in our Lord Jesus Christ, the Lord of glory." James is strengthening his imperative based on the character of the Lord Jesus Christ. The Bible clearly teaches that God does not show partiality (Deut. 10:17; 1 Samuel 16:7; Job 34:19; Romans 2:11; Matthew 22:16). Therefore, it makes sense that those who have placed their faith in Jesus, the Lord of glory, should not show partiality.

- Coach, have there been instances when you showed partiality with your athletes?

If so, confess them to the Lord and ask for His grace to move forward in not showing partiality.

- How can you practically help your athletes to value every member of your team and show no partiality?

___

▶ CONSIDER THE ILLUSTRATION OF PARTIALITY

James emphasizes how serious partiality is by pulling out the game film and showing an illustration. He wants us all to get it. In verses 2-4 James gives an illustration that contrasts the treatment of two different kinds of people who enter a place of corporate worship and how they are treated. The person whose outward appearance indicates wealth is treated with honor. The man whose outward appearance indicates he is poor is treated with dishonor. James says that this kind of behavior is exactly what God commanded them not to do in verse 1. The phrase "evil thoughts (v. 4)" is speaking of "evil motives." Their treatment of the wealthy man with honor exposed their evil motives of thinking they would get something from him in return.

- Coach, have you ever treated an athlete a certain way hoping to get something in return for your own benefit? If so, confess it to God, thank him for the forgiveness you have in Christ and ask him for the power to forsake it.

- When we treat our athletes with favor, or the opposite, based on their outward appearance, we show that our motives are evil and self-seeking. Ask the Lord to empower you to focus on serving your athletes, so they will become the people He desires them to be.

___

▶ REALIZE THE INCONSISTENCY OF PARTIALITY

James points out in verse 5 that God's plan of redemption includes the poor who realize His promise of being "rich in faith and heirs of His kingdom" based on their love for Him (faith in Christ) not on their earthly riches. In verse 6, James teaches that dishonoring the poor, who God honors, is inconsistent with the character of God and therefore, it's inappropriate for someone who has been made new in Christ. James also points out that the rich to whom they were showing favor to, were oppressing the poor and speaking against the Lord Jesus Christ (vv. 6b-7). This once again shows the inconsistency of partiality.

- Coach, how, fueled by your faith in Jesus, can you purposely show honor to all your athletes—not on the basis of their ability but based on the fact they are created in the image of God?

_____
_____
_____

▶ UNDERSTAND THE IMPORTANCE OF PARTIALITY

Many people in James' day, and in ours, want to dismiss the sin of partiality as insignificant. However, in verses 8-11, James shows that the sin of partiality is very important and very serious. James first commends some of the believers and says they are "doing well" for not showing partiality as evidence by the fact that they are loving others as themselves (v. 8). However, there are others who are "committing sin" by showing partiality and thus breaking the law of loving others (v. 9). Some of the people to whom James wrote, as well as some people today would say: "Come on. We're talking about partiality here … It's not like I murdered someone or committed adultery." God through James would say, "Yes, it is like you have committed murder and adultery (v.11)."

- Coach, how can the sin of partiality undermine your ability to reach the heart of your athletes with the Gospel and hinder your call as a coach?

- How can you emphasize the importance and seriousness of the sin of partiality with your athletes?

_____

_____

_____

_____

▶ BE MOTIVATED BY THE IMMINENT JUDGMENT OF PARTIALITY

In verse 12 James emphasizes that as true followers of Christ we are to live our lives continuously in the light of the imminent judgment to come. As those who have been made new in Christ through faith in Him, we will not be judged on whether or not we have eternal life. That is a settled issue. Our judgment is a judgment of reward or lack thereof (2 Corinthians 5:10; 1 Corinthians 3:12-15). In verse 13 James gives a sobering caution concerning the imminent judgment of partiality. The one who shows no mercy possibly reveals a heart that has not received mercy. Those who have received the mercy of God, do not live a life characterized by showing partiality based on outward appearance. Mercy is a fruit of faith in Jesus. James' main point in verses 12-13 is that partiality will be judged, and it should serve as a motivation for us to never, ever show partiality (no mercy). After all we are ones who have been shown infinite mercy in Christ.

- Coach, how can the imminent judgment of partiality motivate you to show mercy (lack of partiality) to your athletes?
- Coach, have you received the mercy of God found through faith in Christ? If so, thank the Lord for giving you the power to keep from showing partiality to your athletes and instead show mercy to all.

_____

_____

_____

GAME CHANGER

As followers of Jesus we must always be reminded that before we were given new life by grace through faith, we were "dead in our trespasses and sins (Ephesians 2:1)" and "enemies of God (Romans 5:10)." Thankfully God did not show partiality to us based on our own unrighteousness. Instead, He showed us mercy and made us His children. Therefore, His mercy toward us, and in us, can empower us to show mercy to others, and to refrain from the sin of partiality.

"But God, being rich in mercy, because of the great love with which he loved us, even when we were dead in our trespasses, made us alive together with Christ—by grace you have been saved." – Ephesians 2:4-5

ONE BIG THING

What is the most significant lesson for you to take with you from this chapter?

___
___
___
___
___
___
___
___
___
___

IMPACT PRAYER

Father, by Your grace, fuel my faith in such a way that I refrain from showing partiality to the athletes You have entrusted to me. Help me see each of them as created in Your image and value them as such. May my actions toward my athletes be consistent with Your character and therefore with the new nature You have given me in Christ. Remind me of the seriousness of partiality and the pain it brings to people. May I extend the mercy You have shown me to all of the athletes You have entrusted to me, regardless of their ability. May all of this bring You glory. In Jesus' name I pray, Amen.

CHAPTER FIVE
THE FAITH-FUELED COACH
AUTHENTIC FAITH

JAMES 2:14-26

STUDY STARTER

As a coach you have most likely dealt with the self-deception of your athletes. Many of your athletes think they are better than they really are. This makes it very difficult to coach them. Without seeing a need to improve they will not be coachable. The consequences of dealing with self-deceived athletes are poor performances by individuals that ultimately hurt the performance of the team. These consequences are minor when compared to the self-deception that takes place in the lives of many people when it comes to their relationship with God. Many people think they have been made right with God when they really have not been. Thinking you are right with God when you really are not, is the difference between eternal life and eternal death. In James 2:14-26, James is going to challenge us to examine our faith to see if it is authentic faith or false faith. God through James does this because He loves us and wants us to know the joy of an authentic faith in Christ that leads to a faith-fueled life. He does not want us to be self-deceived.

STUDY PASSAGE

[14] What good is it, my brothers, if someone says he has faith but does not have works? Can that faith save him? [15] If a brother or sister is poorly clothed and lacking in daily food, [16] and one of you says to them, "Go in peace, be warmed and filled," without giving them the things needed for the body, what good is that? [17] So also faith by itself, if it does not have works, is dead. [18] But someone will say, "You have faith and I have works." Show me your faith apart from your works, and I will show you my faith by my works. [19] You believe that God is one; you do well. Even the demons believe—and shudder! [20] Do you want to be shown, you foolish person, that faith apart from works is useless? [21] Was not Abraham our father justified by works when he offered up his son Isaac on the altar? [22] You see that faith was active along with his works, and faith was completed by his works; [23] and the Scripture was fulfilled that says, "Abraham believed God, and it was

counted to him as righteousness"—and he was called a friend of God. ²⁴ You see that a person is justified by works and not by faith alone. ²⁵ And in the same way was not also Rahab the prostitute justified by works when she received the messengers and sent them out by another way? ²⁶ For as the body apart from the spirit is dead, so also faith apart from works is dead.

STUDY HELP

- **vv. 14, 16 – "*good*"** = advantage or profit.
- **v. 14 – "*save*"** = rescue
- **v. 14 – "*works*"** = actions or deeds performed by someone.
- **vv. 14, 17, 18, 20, 22, 24, 26 – "*faith*"** = a strong confidence in and reliance upon.
- **v. 19 – "*believe*'** = to accept as true or to trust. (Here in v. 19 the former definition is in mind)
- **v. 19 – "*shudder*"** = shiver; bristle up like a frightened cat.
- **v. 20 – "*shown*"** = acknowledge.
- **v. 20– "*foolish*"** = empty.
- **vv. 21, 24, 25 – "*justified*"** = legally pronounce righteous or right (Romans 3:24, 28, 5:1). However, in James 2 it carries the meaning of something being validated as right or true based on proof (Romans 3:4; 1 Timothy 3:16; Matthew 11:19).
- **v. 22 – "*completed*"** = brought to its intended goal; maturity.

EXTRA HELP

It is critical to mention here that in no way is James teaching that it is by faith plus works that a person earns salvation. In these verses, he is not addressing how one comes to faith in Christ but is instead describing the evidence (validation) of one who already possesses an authentic faith in Christ. The main point James is stressing in these verses has been summarized well with the following statement – "We are saved by grace alone through faith alone in Christ alone, but a faith that saves is never alone."

STUDY QUESTIONS

1. According to verse 14, what answer is James assuming to his question of "What good is it, my brothers, if someone says he has faith but does not have works?"

_____

_____

_____

2. According to verse 14, does someone who professes to have faith, but it is not accompanied by works, possess a faith that saves them from the penalty of their sin?

_____

_____

_____

3. Based on vv. 15-17 what kind of faith does a person have if they possess the means to help someone in need, but they do not help and only offer them a verbal blessing? When you see a need on your team (physically, mentally, emotionally, spiritually), does your faith fuel you to seek to meet that need?

_____

_____

_____

4. According vv. 18-20, to whom does James compare those who believe that faith and works do not have to be related (v. 19)? Or what does a mere mental ascent to some facts about God qualify a person to be (v. 19)?

_____

_____

_____

5. Based on vv. 21-24, how was Abraham's faith validated as authentic?

_____
_____

6. Based on v. 25, how was Rahab's faith validated as authentic? What things have you incorporated into your program to help your athletes see that what you do is directly related to your faith in Jesus?

_____
_____
_____

STUDY SUMMARY

God desires for us to have an authentic faith that is validated by our words, actions and attitudes.

COACHING CONNECTION

Coach, an authentic faith in Jesus as Savior and Lord will fuel our lives in such a way that it will show up in the way we coach our athletes.

KEYS TO WINNING

▶ VIDEO GUIDE AT KINGDOMSPORTS.ONLINE

▶ CONSIDER CAREFULLY TWO QUESTIONS

In verse 14 the first question to carefully consider is "What good is it?" The phrase "says he has faith but does not have works" is in the present tense indicating that this type of person repeatedly claims they have a saving faith, but a lack of works characterizes their life. The answer to the question of "What good is it when a person constantly claims faith in Christ, but has no consistent evidence of works in their life?" is a resounding "It's no good," This person's profession of faith is empty.

The second question in verse 14 to carefully consider is "Can that faith save him?" The context of the passage makes it clear that the faith referred to is a faith that has no works. So, the question is not "Can faith save a person?", but rather "Can a faith that produces no works save a person or justify them before God?" And the clear answer here is "No!"

- Coach, how does the faith you profess in Jesus fuel your life in such a way that it is evident to your fellow coaches and athletes?
- I want to challenge you to ask another coach or athlete how they see your faith in Jesus lived out in the way you coach.

_____
_____
_____
_____
_____

▶ CONSIDER TWO ILLUSTRATIONS OF A FALSE FAITH

The first illustration of a false faith is that of a hypocritical compassion (vv. 15-17). James presents a person who notices and speaks words of compassion to someone in extreme poverty. The original Greek words translated for us as "be warmed and filled" point to the fact that this person has no intention of actually meeting the needs at hand. The second half of verse 16 indicates this person had the ability to give what was necessary but was unwilling to meet the need. James then asks the question, "what good is that?" The obvious answer to this question is that it is no good to anyone – it is useless.

The second illustration of a false faith is one of a mental confession (vv. 18-20) in which someone objects to the fact that faith and works are interrelated (v. 18). James' demands for the objector to "Show me your faith apart from your works," which is impossible to do. James also shows the objector that a mere mental confession of some facts about God ("God is one"), only qualifies one to be a demon (v.19). In verse 20 James calls on the objector to recognize that faith apart from works is useless.

- Coach, how can your faith in Jesus fuel you to display true compassion to those you coach?
- Coach, how can you practically teach your athletes the inseparable relationship between faith and works?

_____
_____
_____
_____

▶ CONSIDER TWO ILLUSTRATIONS OF A VALIDATED FAITH

Before considering the two illustrations of a validated faith, it is important to understand that the word justified has two meanings in the New Testament. First, it refers to a legal pronouncement of innocence over a sinner and a declaration that they are righteous (i.e. Romans 3:24, 28, 5:1). This is the root of salvation. The second meaning of 'Justified' is the validation of something as true based on conduct or actions (Romans 3:4; 1 Timothy 3:16; Matthew 11:19). This is the fruit of salvation. In James 2:21-26, James illustrates with the lives of Abraham and Rahab that their faith, which they already possessed, was validated or proven to be authentic by their actions.

- Coach, spend some time in prayer thanking God for the faith to trust in Jesus as your Lord and Savior. Then ask Him to reveal areas in your life and coaching that are not validating your faith in Jesus. Then ask Him to fuel your faith to be evident in all your attitudes and actions.

_____
_____

GAME CHANGER

The Lord Jesus clearly taught that faith and works are related. In John 8:31 we find these words, "So Jesus said to the Jews who had believed him, 'If you abide in my word, you are truly my disciples.'" Jesus was speaking to those who had believed in Him and was teaching that their abiding in or obeying His word validated their faith. Coach, be encouraged that if you have truly placed your faith in Jesus, your faith will lead to a life of growing obedience to His word, which will edify others and glorify God.

ONE BIG THING

What is the most significant lesson for you to take with you from this chapter?

_____
_____
_____
_____
_____
_____
_____

IMPACT PRAYER

Father, by Your grace, fuel my faith in Jesus in such a way that it is on full display when I coach, so that You are glorified. Show me areas in my life and coaching where I need to grow so that my faith in Jesus is more evident. Empower me to effectively and practically teach the athletes You have entrusted to me the inseparable relationship between faith and works. In Jesus' name I pray, Amen.

CHAPTER SIX
THE FAITH-FUELED COACH
THE TONGUE

JAMES 3:1-12

STUDY STARTER

As a coach you understand the powerful impact the words you use can have on your athletes and fellow coaches. No doubt you have personally witnessed how the words you spoke brought hope and encouragement to them. You have also most likely witnessed firsthand how words have discouraged and defeated an athlete or coach. All of us understand the reality of what is recorded in Proverbs 18:21, "Death and life are in the power of the tongue." God wants us to use our words to build up and give life to those we lead as coaches. Thankfully He has much instruction and help for us in James 3:1-12.

STUDY PASSAGE

¹ Not many of you should become teachers, my brothers, for you know that we who teach will be judged with greater strictness. ² For we all stumble in many ways. And if anyone does not stumble in what he says, he is a perfect man, able also to bridle his whole body. ³ If we put bits into the mouths of horses so that they obey us, we guide their whole bodies as well. ⁴ Look at the ships also: though they are so large and are driven by strong winds, they are guided by a very small rudder wherever the will of the pilot directs. ⁵ So also the tongue is a small member, yet it boasts of great things. How great a forest is set ablaze by such a small fire! ⁶ And the tongue is a fire, a world of unrighteousness. The tongue is set among our members, staining the whole body, setting on fire the entire course of life, and set on fire by hell, ⁷ For every kind of beast and bird, of reptile and sea creature, can be tamed and has been tamed by mankind, ⁸ but no human being can tame the tongue. It is a restless evil, full of deadly poison. ⁹ With it we bless our Lord and Father, and with it we curse people who are made in the likeness of God. ¹⁰ From the same mouth come blessing and cursing. My brothers, these things ought not to be so. ¹¹ Does a spring pour forth from the same opening both fresh and salt water? ¹² Can a fig tree, my brothers, bear olives, or a grapevine produce figs? Neither can a salt pond yield fresh water.

STUDY HELP

- v. 1– **"teachers"** = those who instruct.
- v. 2 – **"stumble"** = a failure in duty; sin.
- v. 2 – **"perfect"** = mature; complete.
- v. 2 – **"bridle"** = hold in check.
- v. 3 – **"bit"** = a small piece of metal placed in a horse's mouth used to control the direction of the horse.
- v. 4 – **"very small"** = least; insignificant.
- v. 4 – **"rudder"** = steering oar.
- v. 5 – **"member"** = part of the body.
- v. 6 – **"unrighteousness"** = failure to hold to moral principles.
- v. 6 – **"staining"** = impairing with a flaw.
- vv. 7, 8 – **"tame(d)"** = subdued.
- v. 8 – **"poison"** = venom from a snake.
- vv. 9, 10 – **"bless"** = to express esteem or honor for someone.
- vv. 9, 10 – **"curse"** = to speak against someone

EXTRA HELP

Great respect was given to teachers of God's Word in the early Church, which made it an enviable or desirable position on the surface. James knew that some people only wanted to be teachers for the praise and prestige of the position, without considering the great responsibility that came with it. This is true of the position of a coach as well.

STUDY QUESTIONS

1. According to verse 1, why does James warn against the desire to become a teacher of God's Word? How does this warning impact you as a coach and the things you are teaching your athletes about God's Word through your sport?

2. According to verse 2, what does the ability to control the tongue indicate about a person? What kind of impact have other coaches who are able to control their tongue had on your life?

3. Based on vv. 3-5a what is James' main point about the tongue? Why is this important for you to understand as a coach?

4. Based on vv. 5b-6, in what way does James present the consuming nature of the tongue? What kind of attitude or culture is consuming your team based on the words you, as a coach, are using?

5. Based on vv. 7-8, what does James want us to acknowledge when it comes to taming the tongue?

6. Based on vv. 9-12, what does the inconsistent use of the tongue reveal about someone's heart/mind? Based on the use of your tongue when coaching, what does it reveal about your heart/mind?

STUDY SUMMARY

God desires for us to understand the power of the tongue and to use our words to glorify Him and edify others

COACHING CONNECTION

Coach, our faith in Jesus fuels our life in such a way that our words will be used to build up our athletes instead of tear them down.

KEYS TO WINNING

▶ **VIDEO GUIDE AT KINGDOMSPORTS.ONLINE**

▶ **CONSIDER THE IMPORTANCE OF THE TONGUE**

In verse 1 James emphasizes the importance of the tongue with a warning. James warns that teachers will be judged more strictly; and if you are a teacher for the wrong reason, that judgment will not be pleasant. James gives this warning because of the critical role that speech plays in teaching. The same can be applied to coaching.

In verse 2 James further emphasizes the importance of the tongue by having us consider the fact that the tongue is a struggle for everyone, not just teachers. He also stresses its importance by pointing out that if we can spiritually mature to a point that we can subdue and control it, we can control the rest of our lives as well.

- Coach, how does the warning about how leaders use their tongues impact the way you use yours as you coach

- How have you seen God mature you in the use of your tongue and how has that impacted your relationships with your athletes?

_____
_____
_____
_____
_____

▶ UNDERSTAND THE POWER OF THE TONGUE

In verses 3-4, James uses two illustrations to emphasize the power of the tongue. In verse 3 he shows how a powerful horse can be controlled by a small piece of metal (bit) in its mouth. In verse 4 he shows how a huge ship can be controlled by a small rudder.

James summarizes his two illustrations and relates them to our tongue in the first part of verse 5, "So also the tongue is a small member, yet it boasts of great things." James' point is that just like a small bit controls a large horse and a small rudder controls a large ship, so too does the small tongue control our lives. The tongue can both build up and tear down a person. Proverbs 15:4 highlights this truth: "A gentle tongue is a tree of life, but perverseness in it breaks the spirit."

- Coach, how have you seen the power of the tongue impact the athletes you coach?
- Coach, in what practical ways can you use the power of the tongue to build up your athletes and fellow coaches?

_____
_____
_____
_____
_____

▶ BEWARE OF THE CONSUMING NATURE OF THE TONGUE

In verse 5b and 6 James illustrates the consuming nature of the tongue by likening it to fire. Just like a small spark can consume a whole forest, so too can one small word consume our lives and stain them with unrighteousness.

James continues to show the consuming nature of the tongue when he exposes its source with the words "and is set on fire by hell." The word "hell" (gehenna) means the valley of Hinnom. This place was used in the first century as the garbage dump for the city of Jerusalem where fires burned constantly to destroy the trash it contained. This is a perfect picture of a place where Satan feels right at home. The source of the consuming nature of the tongue is hell itself and if we let him, Satan will influence us to use our tongue as his tool to bring about a consuming fire of destruction in every area of our lives and the lives of others.

- Coach, recall a time when you have seen the consuming nature of the tongue spread through a team. How did it impact that team's performance on and off the field or court?

_____

_____

_____

▶ ACKNOWLEDGE THE TONGUE IS HUMANLY UNTAMABLE

In verses 7-8 James wants us to acknowledge the tongue is humanly untamable. In verse 7 James points out the fact that as humans we have been able to bring under control many kinds of animals for our own purposes. In the second half of verse 8 he describes the tongue "as a restless evil, full of deadly poison." This language compares the tongue to a wild animal trying to escape captivity and a venomous snake (i.e. Psalm 140:3).

Now notice the first phrase in verse 8, "but no human being can tame the tongue." James makes it clear that "no human being" has the natural ability to tame the tongue. It is humanly untamable. I think we can all attest to this truth. We have tried to tame our tongues yet have failed time and time again. God through James wants us to acknowledge this and realize our only hope to tame the tongue is God's empowering grace.

- Coach, to begin to tame the tongue you must first acknowledge that in your own strength this is an impossible task. Take some time to acknowledge this to God and then ask Him to give you His empowering grace to tame your tongue.

- Write down the name of three people you can ask to pray for you regarding the taming of your tongue. Then today, ask each of them to pray for you on this manner consistently.

_____
_____
_____
_____
_____

▶ UNDERSTAND THE TONGUE IS REVEALING

In verses 9-12 James wants us to understand the fact that the tongue is revealing. He begins in verses 9-10 by pointing out the inconsistency in the use of our tongue when we use it to bless and curse. He says this inconsistency of the tongue makes no sense (ought not to be so). Those of us who know Christ have been made new and God, the Holy Spirit, resides in us. Therefore, we have the power to use our tongues to consistently bless God and those He has created.

What does an inconsistent tongue reveal? In verses 11-12 James uses three illustrations to help us understand. In these illustrations James is teaching that the tongue is revealing of the condition of our hearts/minds. A heart/mind that has pollution in it will produce rotten words. A heart/mind that is pure will produce pure words. We must address what is in our hearts/minds, so that our words will consistently bless God and those He has created.

- Coach, what does the use of your tongue reveal about your heart/mind?

- God promises that our lives and tongues can be transformed by the renewing of our minds (Romans 12:2). He does this by renewing our minds daily through His

Word, the Bible. What is your plan to allow His Word to renew your mind so it will overflow into the use of your tongue?

___

GAME CHANGER

Coach, we can all relate to not using our tongue in a way that honors the Lord and builds up those we lead. The encouraging news is that those who have placed their faith in Jesus as their Savior and Lord, have the Spirit of God in them and are new creations with the power to tame the tongue (Ezekiel 36:26; 2 Corinthians 5:17). Make it a consistent practice to fill your heart and mind with the good things of God's Word (Philippians 4:8), rely on God, the Holy Spirit, to guard your heart (Proverbs 4:23) and ask God to guard your tongue (Psalm 141:3).

ONE BIG THING

What is the most significant lesson for you to take with you from this chapter?

___

IMPACT PRAYER

Father, by Your grace, I humbly cry out to You as David did in Psalm 141:3, "Set a guard, O Lord, over my mouth; Keep watch over the door of my lips." Impress on me the importance and the power of the tongue by reminding me of the truth that "Death and life are in the power of the tongue. (Proverbs 18:21)" I confess I have used my tongue in a way that is inconsistent with someone who has been made new through faith in Jesus. Fuel my faith in such a way that I use my tongue to build up those You have called me to lead. In Jesus' name I pray, Amen.

★ ★ ★

CHAPTER SEVEN
THE FAITH-FUELED COACH
WISDOM

JAMES 3:13-18

STUDY STARTER

Do your athletes ever seek wisdom from the wrong sources? Of course, the answer is, yes. They often seek wisdom from people who will lead them astray on and off of the field or court. All the while they have you as a coach who would love to give them good wisdom as it pertains to their sport and life as a whole. Yet, no matter how much wisdom you offer them or how often you let them know you are available to help them work through issues, they still sometimes look to poor sources of wisdom. How about you, coach? Do you ever seek wisdom from the wrong sources? If we are all honest, the answer is, yes. We often seek wisdom from wrong sources, which leads to trouble. Thankfully God, through James, gives us some practical instruction on wisdom and how to discern the right and wrong sources of wisdom.

STUDY PASSAGE

[13] Who is wise and understanding among you? By his good conduct let him show his works in the meekness of wisdom. [14] But if you have bitter jealousy and selfish ambition in your hearts, do not boast and be false to the truth. [15] This is not the wisdom that comes down from above, but is earthly, unspiritual, demonic. [16] For where jealousy and selfish ambition exist, there will be disorder and every vile practice. [17] But the wisdom from above is first pure, then peaceable, gentle, open to reason, full of mercy and good fruits, impartial and sincere. [18] And a harvest of righteousness is sown in peace by those who make peace.

STUDY HELP

- ***v. 13 – "wise & understanding"*** = practical application of knowledge to a moral situation.
- ***v. 13 – "good"*** = beautiful, noble, attractive.
- ***v. 13 – "show"*** = give evidence or proof of.
- ***v. 13 – "meekness"*** = humility; strength under control.
- ***v. 14 – "bitter jealously"*** = envy.
- ***v. 14 – "selfish ambition"*** = one who uses unethical means to promote and pursue their own interests at the expense of others.
- ***v. 15 – "earthly"*** = bound by the things of this world.
- ***v. 15 – "unspiritual"*** = from the mind of sinful mankind.
- ***v. 15 – "demonic"*** = from the devil.
- ***v. 16 – "disorder"*** = instability leading to disunity.
- ***v. 17 – "pure"*** = undefiled.
- ***v. 17 – "peaceable"*** = without conflict internally and externally.
- ***v. 17 – "gentle"*** = one who forgoes their right for the betterment of others.
- ***v. 17 – "open to reason"*** = willing to listen to others and make changes when wrong.
- ***v. 17 – "full of mercy and good fruits"*** = compassion in action.
- ***v. 17 – "impartial"*** = does not show favoritism.
- ***v. 17 – "sincere"*** = authentic

EXTRA HELP

In this passage James is challenging those who consider themselves to be "wise and understanding" to step forward in order that he might examine the legitimacy of their claim. Based on this, it seems that some of the recipients of this letter from James were boasting about their wisdom and understanding. James' definition of wisdom and understanding is opposite of the world's and demands our careful study.

STUDY QUESTIONS

1. According to verse 13, what does James say is the evidence of a person who has "wisdom and understanding?" How can you use this truth to exhort your athletes to pursue true "wisdom and understanding?"

_____
_____
_____

2. According to verse 13, what does the word "meekness" communicate concerning our posture or attitude when displaying wisdom? How can this truth help you in training the leaders on your team?

_____
_____
_____

3. According to v. 14, what is the posture or attitude of those who display 'wisdom that is not from above?' Give an example of when this kind of attitude permeated your own use of wisdom. How did that affect your team?

_____
_____
_____

4. According to verse 16 what are the results of 'wisdom that is not from above?' How can this kind of wisdom impact your team?

_____
_____
_____

5. According to verse 17, which of the characteristics of the 'wisdom from above' stands out to you the most? How would this characteristic practically impact your coaching?

_____
_____
_____

6. According to verse 18 what are the results of the 'wisdom from above?' How can this kind of wisdom impact your team?

_____

_____

_____

STUDY SUMMARY

God desires for us to embrace 'Heavenly Wisdom' that will be a blessing to those around us.

COACHING CONNECTION

Coach, our faith in Jesus fuels our wisdom in such a way that it brings peace and righteousness to the coaches and athletes we lead.

KEYS TO WINNING

▶ **VIDEO GUIDE AT KINGDOMSPORTS.ONLINE**

▶ UNDERSTAND THE DEFINITION OF WISDOM

In verse 13 James uses the words "wisdom" and "understanding" as synonyms with the slight distinction of the fact that "wisdom" denotes a moral quality while "understanding" denotes more of an intellectual quality. These terms go hand in hand leading to action. True wisdom is seen by doing what is good and right (good conduct) with an attitude of humility (meekness).

James understood something very important: "Wisdom is not seen in one's academic degrees, but in one's practical good deeds." He was following Jesus' lead on this when Jesus said, "Everyone then who hears these words of mine and does them will be like a wise man who built his house on the rock (Matthew 7:24)." It is not the acquisition of information that proves wisdom, instead it is the practical application of God's Word that proves wisdom.

- Coach, give an example of how you have seen a coach display "wisdom" with an attitude of "meekness?"
- How would your athletes describe the way you display "wisdom and understanding" in your coaching?

_____
_____
_____
_____
_____

▶ REJECT WORLDLY WISDOM

In verses 14-16 James presents the characteristics, source and results of wordly wisdom and in so doing he calls us, by God's grace, to reject it. Worldly wisdom is characterized by envy (bitter jealousy) and the pursuit of one's own interests at the expense of others (self-ambition). These characteristics of worldly wisdom are the exact opposite of the "meekness" associated with true wisdom (verse 13).

In verse 15 James says that the source of worldly wisdom is in this world (earthly), in the mind of mankind (unspiritual) and comes from the devil (demonic). The Bible tells us in John 8:44 that the devil is "the father of lies." In our passage, James makes it clear that the source of worldly wisdom are the lies that the devil plants in the minds of mankind.

In verse 16, James points to the results of worldly wisdom beginning with "disorder", which we defined earlier as" instability leading to disunity." The second result of worldly wisdom is described by the words "every vile practice." James says that absolutely nothing good results from worldly wisdom.

- Coach, how have you seen worldly wisdom show up within your team or other teams you have witnessed?
- What can you do to ensure that worldly wisdom does not undermine your coaching?

_____
_____
_____
_____
_____

▶ EMBRACE HEAVENLY WISDOM

In verses 17-18 James presents the source, the characteristics and the results of heavenly wisdom and therefore calls us, by God's grace, to embrace it. In verse 17 we see the source of heavenly wisdom is God Himself (wisdom from above).

In the remainder of verse 17, James lists the characteristics of heavenly wisdom. He first writes that heavenly wisdom "is first pure." It is pure in motives, service and relationships. This is the overarching characteristic from which the other characteristics flow. Heavenly wisdom, which is pure, produces people who

- pursue peace (peaceable)

- set aside their rights for the betterment of others (gentle)
- listen to others with a heart to understand (open to reason)
- seek to meet the needs of others (full of mercy and good fruits)
- do not show favoritism (impartial)
- who are authentic (sincere)

In verse 18, James points to the results of heavenly wisdom when he writes, "And a harvest of righteousness is sown in peace by those who make peace." In other words, the peace that flows from heavenly wisdom will lead to the planting of peace in others. This will then produce righteousness in their lives. A coach who displays heavenly wisdom will be a blessing to those he leads.

- Coach, take a moment to review the characteristics of heavenly wisdom listed above. Which of these characteristics have you seen in the lives of other coaches you respect? How did these characteristics impact that coaches' athletes?
- How have you seen heavenly wisdom impact your team?

_____
_____
_____
_____
_____

GAME CHANGER

Coach, do you want to have **heavenly wisdom** permeate your life and the lives of your athletes? The good news is you can. In 1 Corinthians 1:24 we learn that Christ is "the wisdom of God." Therefore, in order to have **heavenly wisdom** we must first know Christ through faith. Once we know Christ, we then have the power to daily live out the **heavenly wisdom** described here in James.

ONE BIG THING

What is the most significant lesson for you to take with you from this chapter?

_____
_____
_____
_____
_____
_____

IMPACT PRAYER

Father, thank You for enabling me to know Christ and therefore have 'Heavenly Wisdom'. By Your grace, remind me that true wisdom is seen in the practical application of Your Word to all of life. Reveal to me areas of my coaching where I am displaying 'Worldly Wisdom' and then empower me to reject those actions and attitudes. Give me a desire to embrace 'Heavenly Wisdom' and the power to live it out so it will be a blessing to the athletes you have given me to lead. In Jesus' name I pray, Amen

NOTES

CHAPTER EIGHT
THE FAITH-FUELED COACH
CONFLICT

JAMES 4:1-10

STUDY STARTER

Coach, have you ever had conflict on your team? We could all answer 'yes' to that question. Do you currently have conflict on your team? Some of us can answer 'yes,' others 'no.' However, if the answer is 'no' now, 'yes' is right around the corner. We all know the damage that conflict (internally and externally) can do to a team, if not handled well. The truth is conflict is an ongoing reality on teams and with people in general. How do we overcome conflict and minimize its damage and occurrences on our teams? Thankfully, God through James is very clear on how to overcome conflict within and among our athletes, coaches and our families.

STUDY PASSAGE

[1] What causes quarrels and what causes fights among you? Is it not this, that your passions are at war within you? [2] You desire and do not have, so you murder. You covet and cannot obtain, so you fight and quarrel. You do not have, because you do not ask. [3] You ask and do not receive, because you ask wrongly, to spend it on your passions. [4] You adulterous people! Do you not know that friendship with the world is enmity with God? Therefore whoever wishes to be a friend of the world makes himself an enemy of God. [5] Or do you suppose it is to no purpose that the Scripture says, "He yearns jealously over the spirit that he has made to dwell in us"? [6] But he gives more grace. Therefore it says, "God opposes the proud but gives grace to the humble." [7] Submit yourselves therefore to God. Resist the devil, and he will flee from you. [8] Draw near to God, and he will draw near to you. Cleanse your hands, you sinners, and purify your hearts, you double-minded. [9] Be wretched and mourn and weep. Let your laughter be turned to mourning and your joy to gloom. [10] Humble yourselves before the Lord, and he will exalt you.

STUDY HELP

- *v. 1* – *"quarrels"* = resentment with hostility.
- *v. 1* – *"fights"* = severe clash; strife.
- *v. 1* – *"passions"* = desires.
- *v. 2* – *"desire"* = lust; a strong want.
- *v. 2* – *"covet"* = envy.
- *v. 3* – *"wrongly"* = in an evil manner.
- *v. 3* – *"spend"* = denotes wasteful spending.
- *v. 4* – *"adulterous people"* = pointing to people unfaithful to God.
- *v. 4* – *"friend"* = a loving relationship that leads to sharing in all things.
- *v. 4* – *"enmity"* = hostile toward another.
- *v. 5* – *"yearns jealously over"* = strong desire for exclusivity.
- *v. 6* – *"grace"* = unmerited favor and the desire and power to do God's will (1 Corinthians 15:10).
- *v. 6* – *"opposes"* = stands against.
- *v. 6* – *"humble"* = a heart attitude of selflessness; lack of pride.
- *v. 7* – *"submit"* = place oneself under the direction and Lordship of God leading to obedience.
- *v. 7* – *"resist"* = withstand.
- *v. 8* – *"double-minded"* = double-souled; trying to go two ways at once.
- *v. 9* – *"wretched"* = miserable; lament.

STUDY QUESTIONS

1. According to verse 1, what is the cause of the conflict going on among those to whom James writes? What does this teach you about the conflict in your life and on your team?

_____

_____

_____

2. According to verse 2, what are the consequences of the conflict going on in verse 1? What consequences have you witnessed on your own team, or other teams, when conflict is present?

_____

_____

_____

3. According to verses 2-3, what is the heart attitude of a person with unresolved conflict and how does it affect his/her prayers? How have you seen a wrong heart attitude affect your prayers?

_____

_____

_____

4. In verse 4, what two words does James use to describe those who follow after their own desires instead of God's desires for them? What is God's desire for us according to verse 5?

_____

_____

_____

5. According to verses 6-8a, what cure does James give for the cause and consequences of our conflict? How can you point your athletes to this cure for conflict in their lives and on the team?

_____

_____

_____

6. According to verses 8b-10 what actions do we need to take to allow God's empowering grace (1 Corinthians 15:10) to bring about His cure for our conflicts? How can you practically emphasize the value of humility on your team?

_____

_____

_____

STUDY SUMMARY

God desires for us to humbly embrace His grace in order to overcome conflict and bring peace in our lives and in the lives of our athletes.

COACHING CONNECTION

Coach, our faith in Jesus fuels our ability to humble our hearts and receive God's grace to overcome conflict in our lives and on our teams.

KEYS TO WINNING

▶ **VIDEO GUIDE AT KINGDOMSPORTS.ONLINE**

▶ ACKNOWLEDGE THE CAUSE OF CONFLICT

In verse 1 James asks two questions regarding conflict. Both of them are rhetorical. The first question is diagnostic, and the second question answers the first.

The first question assumes there are quarrels and fights happening among the people to whom James writes. There are also quarrels and fights happening on our teams and in our families. In order to overcome a problem, you first have to acknowledge there is a problem. If we are ever to overcome conflict, we must acknowledge it exists in our lives.

The second question in verse 1 actually answers the first: What is the cause of our conflict? James says it is our "passions" that "are at war within" us. The war going on within us is a war between the unredeemed flesh and the New Man or New Creation (2 Corinthians 5:21). Here is the picture: As followers of Jesus, the Spirit of God residing in us is prompting us to practice righteousness (specifically peace and harmony with others), while the flesh is prompting us to practice unrighteousness (quarrels and fights with others). We must acknowledge the cause of our conflict is internal. We are therefore responsible for how we deal with this war.

- Coach, what specific conflicts do you see on your team? Internally and with each other?

- How can you help your athletes acknowledge the conflict and take responsibility for it?

_____

_____

_____

_____

▶ UNDERSTAND THE CONSEQUENCES OF CONFLICT

In verse 2 James begins to describe the consequences that come into our lives when we allow the negative desires that are at war within us to win the battle. It is important that we understand the consequences of losing the conflict within.

Notice the progression in verse 2 – Desire leads to Actions (murder/fight and quarrel) and this leads to negative Consequences. God's Word teaches us that our greatest desire should be to bring glory to God in all things (1 Corinthian's 10:31). When glorifying God is our greatest desire it results in God honoring actions which leads to positive consequences (love, joy, peace, trust). Anytime another desire supersedes glorifying God, it results in sinful actions which lead to negative consequences (anxiousness, guilt, fear, depression).

In addition to the natural consequences of our sinful actions, James points to even more serious negative consequences of losing our internal battle: a self-centered attitude that hinders our prayers (v.2b-3) … and the shifting of our allegiance from God to the world, pitting us against God (v.4).

- Coach, how does understanding the consequences of losing the conflict within motivate you to change?
- How can helping your athletes understand the consequences of their actions motivate them?

_____
_____
_____

▶ EMBRACE THE CURE FOR CONFLICT

In verse 5 we see that God's abundant love is focused towards us. He is jealous for our good, because He knows that our greatest good is being wholly devoted to Him. This is the first thing we need to embrace in order to overcome the conflict within us.

In verse 5, we also discover the foundational cure for conflict in the phrase "But he gives more grace." Even when we lose the battle within, which brings negative consequences, God gives us more grace. He gives us grace (desire and power to do His will) to walk through the consequences and win the next battle. No matter your struggle, God promises His grace to overcome it. Embrace His grace as the cure for conflict.

In verses 6-10, James tells us how to embrace God's grace to overcome conflict. We must humble ourselves before the Lord (vv. 6, 10), submit to His will (v. 7), resist the devil (v.7), draw near to God (v. 8) and repent (v. 9). Then His grace enables us to overcome the conflict within, which brings Him glory.

- Coach, what about God's character in verses 5-10 motivates you to want to embrace His cure for the conflict in your life?
- How can God's love and grace toward you fuel the way you coach your athletes to work through internal and external conflict?

_____
_____
_____
_____
_____

GAME CHANGER

Coach, in order to overcome the internal and external conflict in your life you must realize you cannot do it in your own strength. However, if you are rightly related to God through faith in Christ, the Holy Spirit will empower you to overcome the conflict you experience each day. Paul makes this clear when he writes, "But by the grace of God I am what I am, and his grace toward me was not in vain. On the contrary, I worked harder than any of them, though it was not I, but the grace of God that is with me (1 Corinthians 15:10)."

ONE BIG THING

What is the most significant lesson for you to take with you from this chapter?

_____
_____
_____
_____
_____
_____
_____

IMPACT PRAYER

Father, I acknowledge that there is a daily conflict in my life and I am responsible for how I handle that conflict. I also understand that how I handle the conflict has consequences for me and for those around me. I know I cannot win this battle in my own strength. Thank You for Your empowering grace that enables me to win the battle. Empower me daily to embrace Your grace, so that You will be glorified, and my family, fellow coaches and athletes will be blessed. In Jesus' name I pray, Amen.

NOTES

★ ★ ★

CHAPTER NINE
THE FAITH-FUELED COACH
PRIDE – PART 1

JAMES 4:11-17

STUDY STARTER

Coach, who do you consider first in your program? You or others? Who do your athletes consider first? Themselves or others on the team? Social media today shows that people consider themselves first. We have become self-promoters. Pride, having an exaggerated opinion of oneself, has crept in. Pride is the opposite of humility. Humility is an integral part of a fulfilled life, family and team. Humility puts others first and seeks the best for others above self. A person with pride in their heart puts themselves first and does what is best for them at the expensive of others. This kind of pride can destroy a team. The Lord, through James, wants us to recognize the pride in ourselves and in our athletes and root it out for His glory.

STUDY PASSAGE

[11] Do not speak evil against one another, brothers, The one who speaks against a brother or judges his brother, speaks evil against the law and judges the law. But if you judge the law, you are not a doer of the law but a judge. [12] There is only one lawgiver and judge, he who is able to save and to destroy. But who are you to judge your neighbor? [13] Come now, you who say, "Today or tomorrow we will go into such and such a town and spend a year there and trade and make a profit"— [14] yet you do not know what tomorrow will bring. What is your life? For you are a mist that appears for a little time and then vanishes. [15] Instead you ought to say, "If the Lord wills, we will live and do this or that." [16] As it is, you boast in your arrogance. All such boasting is evil. [17] So whoever knows the right thing to do and fails to do it, for him it is sin.

STUDY HELP

- **v. 11 – "speak evil against"** = speak critically; to speak down on; defame or denigrate.
- **v. 11 – "law"** = Leviticus 19:16,18; royal law, the law of love (James 2:8); law of liberty (James 2:12).
- **v. 12 – "neighbor"** = one who is near. The context points to one who is near spiritually; a fellow Christian.
- **v. 13 – "trade"** = engage in business.
- **v. 14 – "mist"** = vapor; insubstantial.
- **v. 14 – "vanishes"** = gone as if you were never here.
- **v. 16 – "evil"** = same word used for the actions of the devil.

EXTRA HELP

In James 4:1-10 we learned that we can only gain victory over the temptations of this world through God's grace that comes when we are humble. Pride is the opposite of humility. In James 4:11 – 5:6, James will give 3 examples of how pride can manifest itself in our lives (speaking down on, presumptuousness and covetousness).

STUDY QUESTIONS

1. According to verse 11, what does James prohibit when speaking about others? Do you, other coaches or athletes use this kind of speech toward others? If so, how does it impact your team?

_____
_____
_____

2. What does Jesus say regarding the law and how we are to view and treat others (Matthew 22:37-40)? How does this relate to James' admonition in verse 11?

_____

_____

_____

3. According to verses 11-12, when someone speaks evil against or down on someone else, who are they ultimately setting themselves above and offending?

_____

_____

_____

4. What is wrong with the type of planning described in verses 13-14? How can this reality help you as you make plans and goals for your team?

_____

_____

_____

5. According to verse 15, what is the most important thing we can do when considering our plans? How do you incorporate God's will into your plans for your team?

_____

_____

_____

6. What kind of impact do the words James uses in verse 16 have on you in regards to being presumptuous (planning your life without considering God's plan)? How does this motivate you to help train your athletes in considering God in all they do?

_____

_____

_____

7. According to verse 17, what is the "right thing to do" based on the context? What is the "right thing to do" for you and your athletes concerning a presumptuous attitude?

_____
_____
_____

STUDY SUMMARY

God desires you and your team to humbly use words that edify instead of crucify and to consider His will in all that you do.

COACHING CONNECTION

Coach, our faith in Jesus fuels our ability to humble ourselves in order to bless others and glorify Him.

KEYS TO WINNING

▶ **VIDEO GUIDE AT KINGDOMSPORTS.ONLINE**

▶ UNDERSTAND THE PRIDE BEHIND SPEAKING DOWN ON

Notice the phrase in verse 11: "Do not speak evil against one another, brothers." To speak evil against means to literally "speak down on", to speak critically in order to influence others to devalue someone. The one doing the "speaking down on" has adopted a superior and prideful position. "Speaking down on" someone else often presents itself in the form of sarcasm. When we speak down on another person we are proud and therefore God opposes us. HE stands against us.

- Coach, in what specific ways have you seen "speaking down on" happen on your team?
- How can you help your team understand and acknowledge the pride behind "speaking down on" others?

_____
_____
_____
_____

▶ UNDERSTAND THE SERIOUSNESS OF SPEAKING DOWN ON

James stresses in multiple ways the seriousness of "speaking down on" others. First, in verse 11, notice that James uses the word brother three times, emphasizing that the one being spoken against when we "speak against" them is a fellow follower of Jesus. When we speak against a fellow believer, we are speaking against someone whom God in Christ has "spoken for." God through the death, burial and resurrection of Christ has spoken in favor of the person we are "speaking against."

The second way in which James stresses the seriousness of "speaking down on" others is by pointing out that when a person "speaks down on" another they are speaking against the law and judging the law? How so? Earlier in James he refers to the royal law (2:8). To "speak down on" is equal to speaking against and judging the law as something that is invalid, unnecessary and not applicable. It is setting yourself above the law as judge, instead of below it – in submission to it.

In verse 12 James again points to the seriousness of "speaking down on" by pointing to the fact that God is the Lawgiver and Judge and only He has the right to sit as Judge and make the final judgment on people. When we "speak down on" another, we are basically setting ourselves up in the place of God as ruler and judge. This is the epitome of pride.

- Coach, how can you help your coaches and athletes understand the seriousness of "speaking down on" others in your program?

_____
_____
_____
_____
_____

▶ UNDERSTAND THE PRIDE BEHIND PRESUMPTUOUSNESS

Presumptuousness is planning your life without considering God's plan. In verses 13 and 14 James presents two symptoms of presumptuousness that expose pride. The first symptom of presumptuousness found in verse 13 is overestimating our ability to control things (Today or tomorrow we will go into such and such a town and spend a year there and trade and make a profit). The second symptom of presumptuousness found in verse 14 is the failure to recognize your frailty (a mist that appears for a little time and then vanishes).

When we overestimate our ability to control things and fail to recognize our frailty ... and then fail to consider God in our plans, then we are basically placing ourselves on the throne of our lives – which is pride.

- Coach, in what ways have you been prideful in overestimating your ability to control things and failing to recognize your frailty?
- How can you practically begin to consider God in all areas of your plans for your program?

_____
_____
_____
_____
_____

▶ ACKNOWLEDGE THE SOVEREIGNTY OF GOD INSTEAD OF THE PRIDE OF PRESUMPTUOUSNESS

Consider the following words in verse 15, "Instead you ought to say, 'If the Lord wills, we will live and do this or that.'" In these words James challenges us to embrace the sovereignty of God in all things. The Lord alone is in control, He alone is sovereign and when we begin to truly acknowledge this we will begin to conquer the pride of presumptuousness.

James highlights the sin of presumptuousness in verses 16 -17 first by saying that a failure to acknowledge the sovereignty of God in all things is boasting and "all such boasting is evil." He also says the "right thing to do" is to acknowledge the sovereignty of God in all things and a failure to do so is "sin."

- Coach, take some time to confess to the Lord your struggle with wanting to control things and not practically acknowledge God's sovereignty over all things including your program?

- How can you help your athletes acknowledge God's sovereignty over their lives and athletic careers?

_____
_____
_____
_____

GAME CHANGER

Coach, we all struggle with the pride of "speaking down on" and "presumptuousness." The solution to overcome these areas of pride is found back in James 4:6 with the words, "But He gives more grace. Therefore, it says, "God opposes the proud but gives grace to the humble." The ability to humble ourselves and receive more of God's empowering grace to overcome pride is available to all those who have trusted in the death, burial and resurrection of Jesus. Instead of pridefully living for ourselves, Jesus made it possible that we could humble ourselves and live for Him.

[14] For the love of Christ controls us, because we have concluded this: that one has died for all, therefore all have died; [15] and he died for all, that those who live might no longer live for themselves but for him who for their sake died and was raised. – 2 Corinthians 5:14-15

ONE BIG THING

What is the most significant lesson for you to take with you from this chapter?

_____
_____
_____
_____
_____
_____
_____

IMPACT PRAYER

Father, I acknowledge that I have spoken down on others in order to lift myself up. I also acknowledge that I have made decisions and plans without acknowledging You and Your sovereignty over all things. By Your grace, help me humble myself before You so that I lift up others and always consider Your will in the decisions and plans I make. In Jesus' name I pray, Amen.

CHAPTER TEN
THE FAITH-FUELED COACH
PRIDE – PART 2

JAMES 5:1-6

STUDY STARTER

Coach, have you ever found yourself desiring the possessions or position of another coach? Desiring the possessions or position of others distracts us from fulfilling the call God has on our lives. This is covetousness and is a sign of pride because we think that God is holding out on us and therefore, He alone is not enough. Covetousness can cripple our ability to be effective and fulfilled in our role as coaches. Thankfully God through James addresses the pride of covetousness, so that we can be rescued from this sin and its consequences in our lives.

STUDY PASSAGE

¹ Come now, you rich, weep and howl for the miseries that are coming upon you. ² Your riches have rotted and your garments are moth-eaten. ³ Your gold and silver have corroded, and their corrosion will be evidence against you and will eat your flesh like fire. You have laid up treasure in the last days. ⁴ Behold, the wages of the laborers who mowed your fields, which you kept back by fraud, are crying out against you, and the cries of the harvesters have reached the ears of the Lord of hosts. ⁵ You have lived on the earth in luxury and in self-indulgence. You have fattened your hearts in a day of slaughter. ⁶ You have condemned and murdered the righteous person. He does not resist you.

STUDY HELP

- *v. 1 – "weep"* = sobbing aloud.
- *v. 1 – "howl"* = wail to express violent grief in the face of judgment.
- *v. 1 – "miseries"* = great distress of the imminent and impending judgment of God against sin.
- *v. 3 – "last days"* = days between Jesus' first and second comings.
- *v. 4 – "kept back by fraud"* = they never intended to pay.
- *v. 4 – "Lord of hosts"* = Lord of the angelic armies.
- *v. 5 – "luxury"* = living a pampered life.
- *v. 5 – "self-indulgence"* = unrestrained excess given to self.
- *v. 5 – "slaughter"* = points to judgment day.
- *v. 6 – "condemned"* = to pervert justice.

EXTRA HELP

In Chapter 9 (James 4:11-17) we examined two of James' examples of how pride can manifest itself in our lives (speaking down on and presumptuousness). In this lesson covering James 5:1-6 we will discover the third example of pride (covetousness). In verses 1-6, James is using a rhetorical device known as apostrophe—the turning away from his real audience to address some other group. His real audience is a group of Christians who are being persecuted by some ungodly rich people. James addresses these ungodly rich people for the benefit of the Christians who might begin to covet or envy the possessions, power, privileges, and prestige of the ungodly rich. Let me be clear as we examine these verses that God does not see wealth in this world as something wrong. It is the pursuit of wealth in the place of God that is wrong and prideful.

STUDY QUESTIONS

1. According to verse 1, why should the ungodly rich weep and howl? What does this teach about how we should view the consequences of our sin?

_____

_____

_____

2. Based on verse 2, what is the ultimate outcome of the treasures of this world? How can you use this to teach your athletes about the importance of pursuing the right treasures?

_____

_____

_____

3. According to verse 3, what is the evidence that a person has made the treasures of this world their ultimate pursuit? What are the consequences of making the treasures of this world your ultimate pursuit?

_____

_____

_____

4. According to verse 4, what two witnesses are there against the ungodly rich and their pursuit of worldly wealth at any cost? Could your athletes or other coaches witness against your unhealthy pursuit of the fame or fortune of this world? If so, why?

_____

_____

_____

_____

5. According to verses 5-6, what is the end for the ungodly rich who mistreat others to acquire the treasures of this world? How should this motivate you to teach your athletes to pursue the right kind of treasures?

___

STUDY SUMMARY

God desires you and your team to see the Lord Jesus Christ as your greatest treasure and not believe the lie that He is holding out on you.

COACHING CONNECTION

Coach, our faith in Jesus fuels our ability to desire Jesus above all earthly treasure.

KEYS TO WINNING

▶ **VIDEO GUIDE AT KINGDOMSPORTS.ONLINE**

▶ REJECT COVETING BECAUSE EARTHLY TREASURES WILL NOT LAST

Look with me at verse 1 and the words "weep" and "howl." These words are used in relation to the judgment of God. James calls the ungodly rich to cry out in despair, because of the "miseries that are coming upon" them. The miseries spoken of here are the imminent and impending judgments of God against their sin. This is the destiny of those that make earthly riches their chief pursuit.

In verses 2-3a James points to three forms of wealth that were held in high esteem: food, clothing, and precious metals. These ungodly rich cling to these worldly riches in order to give them worth, power and prestige in this life—but they will do them no good in the next life. They will be no more. This is the destiny of earthly riches.

Followers of Jesus have no reason to covet the ungodly rich of this world, because we know the destiny of earthly riches they pursue.

- Coach, has the pride of covetousness crept into your coaching career? Why is it folly to covet those who pursue and acquire the highest positions and greatest possessions that can come from coaching?
- How can you help your team understand the destiny of earthly riches?

_____
_____
_____
_____
_____

▸ REJECT COVETING BECAUSE GOD WILL EVENTUALLY JUDGE IT

Look at the second half of verse 3 where James writes, "and their corrosion will be evidence against you and will eat your flesh like fire. You have laid up treasure in the last days." The corrosion being evidence against them is speaking of the fact that the ungodly rich hoarded things when there were those around them who had real needs. This evidence against them will eat their flesh like fire. This is pointing to the lake of fire (Revelation 20:14-15), which is the place where those who reject the Lord Jesus will be placed. This is the fate of those who place their trust in the treasures of this life instead of trusting the Lord Jesus for salvation.

Now look with me at what James writes in the first half of verse 4, "Behold, the wages of the laborers who mowed your fields, which you kept back by fraud, are crying out against you." These ungodly rich were having the common day laborers work hard in their fields all day long and then were not paying them. In fact, the way this is worded indicates they had no intention to ever pay them. This is "fraud." James even paints a picture of the money sitting in their bank accounts that should have been paid to the workers "crying out against" them.

Not only is the money that should have been paid to the laborers crying out, but notice the other cry against the ungodly rich who are committing fraud in the remainder of verse 4; "and the cries of the harvesters have reached the ears of the Lord of hosts." The workers were crying out and their cries had reached the ears of the Lord of hosts. The point James is making is that these ungodly rich landowners had committed fraud against the poor and this injustice had reached the ears of the Almighty God of all the universe who will avenge them.

- Coach, how can you help your coaches and athletes understand the fate of placing their trust in the treasures of this life?

- Are there things your athletes have earned (playing time, encouragement, leadership position) that you are withholding from them? If so, make things right by doing the right thing by them.

- How can you practically help your team understand that when we sin against others, we are ultimately sinning against God?

▶ REJECT COVETING BECAUSE IT ULTIMATELY LEADS TO DEATH AND DESTRUCTION

Notice the first half of verse 5 where James writes, "You have lived on the earth in luxury and in self-indulgence." The word luxury is speaking of a pampered life. Not only did they defraud the poor, but they took the money that should have gone to the poor and used it to live a life of pampered luxury. The word self-indulgence indicates unrestrained self-indulgence in pleasure. This is the same picture presented with the prodigal son, "he squandered his property in reckless living (Luke 15:13)."

Look now at the second half of verse 5 where James writes, "You have fattened your hearts in a day of slaughter." By using this phrase, James is pointing out that the central focus (heart) in the ungodly rich's life is to indulge in the luxuries of this world in a search for satisfaction. Instead of being satisfied they are preparing their hearts for the day of slaughter. James is saying these ungodly rich seek for satisfaction in the things of this world, but instead will get slaughtered – eternal death separated from God forever.

Notice the first part of verse 6, "You have condemned and murdered the righteous person." The ungodly rich were using the court system (which they owned) to condemn the poor so they could not speak against them. James also says they had murdered the righteous person. This could be a literal death sentence that was handed down by the courts that were ruled by the wealthy. It could also mean that the rich had taken away the means of the poor to make a living—which would be like a death sentence. James then writes, "He does not resist you." This speaks to the fact that the poor were not using unethical means to protect themselves but were instead trusting God and honoring HIM even when they were being unjustly abused. This added weight to the guilt of the ungodly rich.

- Coach, in what ways have you allowed the pride of covetousness to lead you to seek luxury over love for the Lord and others? Take some time now to confess this to the Lord.

- As a coach how have you experienced the reality that winning on the scoreboard can ultimately leave you unsatisfied?

- How can pride of covetousness prevent you from being fulfilled?

GAME CHANGER

Coach, no doubt we have all battled the pride of coveting what others have. Once again, the solution to overcome these areas of pride is found back in James 4:6 with the words, "But he gives more grace. Therefore, it says, "God opposes the proud but gives grace to the humble." When we are consistently being reminded of His grace and walking in it, He reminds us that far from holding out on us He has given us the greatest treasure of all—Jesus.

"But whatever gain I had, I counted as loss for the sake of Christ. Indeed, I count everything as loss because of the surpassing worth of knowing Christ Jesus my Lord. For his sake I have suffered the loss of all things and count them as rubbish, in order that I may gain Christ and be found in him." – Philippians 3:7-9a

ONE BIG THING

What is the most significant lesson for you to take with you from this chapter?

_____
_____
_____
_____
_____
_____
_____

IMPACT PRAYER

Father, I acknowledge that I have coveted the things of others in coaching. In doing so I have believed the lie that You are holding out on me, and You alone are not enough. Remind me of your abundant grace toward me in giving me Jesus as my Savior and Lord. Help me daily find my greatest treasure in knowing Jesus more. In Jesus name I pray, Amen.

★★★
CHAPTER ELEVEN
THE FAITH-FUELED COACH
PATIENCE IN DIFFICULTY

JAMES 5:7-12

STUDY STARTER

In order to be a great coach one of the key characteristics we need to develop is patience. We need patience at home, with our athletes, with our fellow coaches, etc. … The good news is the Lord is so committed to developing patience in us that He graciously sends to us difficulties like tribulation, pain, persecution, and disappointment. This may include persecution for your stand for Christ, decisions about playing time or how you handle discipline on your team. Whatever the circumstance—the Lord desires that we be patient so that He is glorified, others are blessed, and we experience the peaceful joy that comes through patience.

STUDY PASSAGE

[7] Be patient, therefore, brothers, until the coming of the Lord. See how the farmer waits for the precious fruit of the earth, being patient about it, until it receives the early and the late rains. [8] You also, be patient. Establish your hearts, for the coming of the Lord is at hand. [9] Do not grumble against one another, brothers, so that you may not be judged; behold, the Judge is standing at the door. [10] As an example of suffering and patience, brothers, take the prophets who spoke in the name of the Lord. [11] Behold, we consider those blessed who remained steadfast. You have heard of the steadfastness of Job, and you have seen the purpose of the Lord, how the Lord is compassionate and merciful. [12] But above all, my brothers, do not swear, either by heaven or by earth or by any other oath, but let your "yes" be yes and your "no" be no, so that you may not fall under condemnation.

STUDY HELP

- **v. 7 – "patient"** = *long-tempered; long fused: it denotes an attitude of self-restraint which keeps a person from hasty retaliation.*
- **v. 7 – "coming"** = *arrival of a king (namely Jesus in this context). This would be something for which these persecuted Christians longed.*
- **v. 7 – "waits"** = *looks expectantly.*
- **v. 8 – "establish your hearts"** = *an attitude of commitment to keep going no matter how severe the trial.*
- **v. 9 – "grumble"** = *criticism and faultfinding directed against others.*
- **v. 10 – "prophets"** = *these were not just the writing prophets, but men sent from God to communicate His truth to the people.*
- **v. 11 – "steadfast"** = *to remain faithful under the difficult circumstances of life.*

EXTRA HELP

In verse 7 James uses the word "therefore" to point back to verses 1-6 which dealt with the persecution of poor believers by the ungodly rich. In light of this, he is now going to implore believers to respond with patience when they face various difficulties in their lives.

STUDY QUESTIONS

1. According to verse 7, what does James exhort the believers to do in the midst of difficulty? What motivation does he give them to embrace this exhortation?

_____
_____
_____

2. Based on verse 7, how would the illustration of a farmer help them to embrace James' exhortation to be patient?

_____
_____
_____

3. According to verse 9, what does James call these believers to avoid in the midst of their difficulties? What is the motivation for not grumbling?

_____
_____
_____

4. In verses 10-11, what examples does James give for being patient in difficulty? What examples of being patient in difficulty would be an encouragement to your athletes?

_____
_____
_____

5. According to verse 12, what does James tell these believers to refrain from in the midst of difficulties? What does truth telling, or non-truth telling, do to the unity and cohesion of your team?

_____
_____
_____

STUDY SUMMARY

God desires you and your team to be patient in difficulty so that He is glorified, and others are edified by your example.

COACHING CONNECTION

Coach, our faith in Jesus fuels our ability to be patient in difficulty.

KEYS TO WINNING

▶ **VIDEO GUIDE AT KINGDOMSPORTS.ONLINE**

▶ EMBRACE THE CALL TO BE PATIENT IN DIFFICULTY

In verse 7, James exhorts these persecuted believers, and us, to be patient when faced with difficulties. Instead of having a 'short fuse' towards people who wrong us and therefore exploding on them – we are to have a 'long fuse' towards those who wrong us. In other words, God through James exhorts us to embrace the call of being patient in difficulty.

In the remainder of verses 7-8 James presents 3 important truths to help us better embrace this call of being patient in difficulty. The 1st truth is the motivation to be patient in difficulty. Notice the phrases in verse 7 and 8: "until the coming of the Lord (v. 7)" and "for the coming of the Lord is at hand (v.8)." When we undergo difficulty, knowing the Lord will return brings comfort and is a great motivation to be patient or have a 'long fuse'.

The second truth to help us be patient in difficulty comes from James in the form of an illustration. We see this in the second half of verse 7 when he writes, "See how the farmer waits for the precious fruit of the earth, being patient about it, until it receives the early and the late rains." James uses the illustration of a farmer who understands there must be a process of growth and development before he can expect to receive a fruitful crop. Just like the farmer waits for the process of farming to be complete, we must wait and expectantly submit to the Lord's work in us through our difficulties, trusting in His goodness to bring about fruit in our lives.

Now look with me at the remainder of verse 8: "Establish your hearts, for the coming of the Lord is at hand." Here we discover the third truth that will help us embrace the call of being patient in difficulty: the determination in patience. The word establish means to have an attitude to keep going no matter the difficulty. As we seek to keep going in the face of difficulty, we trust the Lord is establishing our hearts, so that we will be determined no matter the difficulty.

- Coach, what impact have you seen on your team when you have a 'short fuse' or lack patience?

- How does the fact that the Lord Jesus is coming again motivate you to be patient in the midst of your difficulty?

- What steps can you take to help your athletes learn to be patient in their difficulties?

_____
_____
_____
_____
_____
_____
_____

▶ REFUSE TO GRUMBLE WHILE BEING PATIENT IN DIFFICULTY

In verse 9 James exhorts these believers to "not grumble against one another." The difficulty these Christians were undergoing was influencing some of them to have a short fuse and turn on each other with words that tear down. These attitudes and words are directed at the people who they love the most. James exhorts them to stop.

Now look at verse 9 where James gives us some motivation to not grumble against each other with the words "so that you may not be judged." James is clearly addressing followers of Jesus here (brothers); therefore, he is speaking about the Judgment seat of Christ. This is where believers are rewarded for the way in which they have faithfully served Christ (Romans 14:10-12; 2 Corinthians 5:10; 1 Corinthians 3:10-15; James 1:12) James is warning these Christians that if they turn on each other with grumbling when undergoing difficulty, they will face judgment and lose rewards.

Now look at the last phrase in verse 9: "behold, the Judge is standing at the door." This pictures the Judge (Jesus) about to push the doors open and enter the judgment hall. This is meant to stress the imminence of the judgment and serve to motivate the believers to encourage one another and speak kindly to one another in the midst of their difficulty. In verse 9 we clearly see James exhort us to refuse to grumble while being patient in difficulty.

- Coach, how have you seen grumbling among your athletes or coaches impact your team?

- What can you do to help promote words that build up your team and prevent grumbling (words that tear down)?

- Have you had a grumbling attitude when it comes to your team? Take some time to confess this to the Lord and ask him to change your attitude and empower you to lead your team in a way that builds them up.

▶ FOLLOW THE EXAMPLE OF BEING PATIENT IN DIFFICULTY

In verse 10 James points to the prophets of the Old Testament who spoke in the name of the Lord as examples of being patient in difficulty. Consider Moses who fled Egypt, only to return and be persecuted by Pharaoh and eventually by his own people. Consider David who was continually hunted by Saul. Jeremiah was beaten and put in stocks, imprisoned and thrown in an empty water cistern to sink in the mud. Ezekiel, Daniel and Hosea were all persecuted greatly.

This difficulty does not stop in the New Testament for those who spoke in the name of the Lord. John the Baptist was beheaded, and in the book of Acts we see many of Jesus' Apostles experience persecution. All of these "prophets" suffered greatly for speaking in the name of the Lord. Not only does James say they were examples of suffering, but he says that in the midst of this suffering they were examples of patience—they had a 'long fuse' and trusted God in the midst of their suffering. James presents all of these "prophets" as examples in order for us to find encouragement and hope in difficulty, so we too will be patient in difficulty.

- Coach, what coach has been an example to you of someone who has been patient in difficulty? How does their example encourage you to do the same?

- Coach, take some time to share with your athletes some examples of those who have been patient in difficulty. Also, ask them to share some examples from their own experiences.

_____
_____
_____
_____
_____

▶ UNDERSTAND THE LORD'S PURPOSE OF BEING PATIENT IN DIFFICULTY

Look with me at the first phrase of verse 11: "Behold, we consider those blessed who remained steadfast." Why would we consider people who remained steadfast, blessed? James is going to tell us 'why' in the remainder of the verse. The "those" to whom he is referring looks back to the prophets in verse 10, but in a greater way looks forward to the person introduced next with the phrase: "You have heard of the steadfastness of Job" (Job 1:21).

Is there a greater example (outside of Jesus) in the entire Bible of being steadfast in the midst of difficulty than Job? The book of Job begins by presenting Job as a man who prospered in every way. Satan, believing Job only worshipped God because of the prosperity God had given him, asks God if he can have a crack at Job. God essentially says, "Go for it, but you cannot take his life." God allows Satan to bring calamity on Job's family and on Job's health. Most of the rest of the book of Job consists of Job's three so-called friends who do not give him much encouragement or wisdom. At times, Job complained about his situation, but he never renounced God or abandoned his faith in God. Then God reveals Himself to Job and Job, because of his great suffering and patient endurance through it, knew God in a greater and deeper way than he ever had before his suffering.

Let me ask again, why would we consider people who remained steadfast, blessed? Look at the end of verse 11: "and you have seen the purpose of the Lord, how the Lord is compassionate and merciful." The Lord's purpose for Job's difficulties was so that Job could know in a deeper way that the Lord is compassionate and merciful. We consider people blessed who remain steadfast through difficulty, because we understand that the Lord's purpose in their difficulties is that His children can know Him more fully and be conformed more and more into the image of Jesus (Romans 8:29).

- Coach, how does understanding the Lord's purpose in difficulty help you be patient?

- How can you help your team understand the Lord's purpose in difficulty? What impact would this understanding have on your team when they face difficulty together?

▶ SPEAK TRUTH WHILE BEING PATIENT IN DIFFICULTY

In verse 12 James points to a common practice in his day to try to alleviate difficulty by making rash promises and then not keeping them due to a technicality. This was a deceptive and untruthful practice that James needed to address.

James is addressing the very problem Jesus dealt with in Matthew 5:33-37. The Pharisees basically said that as long as you don't make an oath in God's name then it wasn't really a binding oath. You didn't need to keep it, especially if it wasn't going to turn out in your favor. So, instead of making an oath in God's name, they came up with other things by which to make oaths, such as: heaven, earth, Jerusalem, or your head. In Matthew 23:16-22 we find that they would swear or make oaths in the name of the gold of the temple, the altar or the temple itself. They made it sound like they were serious about their word when they were really only giving themselves a way out later if things didn't go their way. Jesus response to this practice was and still is, "Let what you say be simply 'Yes' or 'No'; anything more than this comes from evil."

Based on the fact God the Father is the truth, Jesus is the truth, and the Holy Spirit is referred to as the Spirit of truth—He calls us to speak the truth. Not only does He call us to speak the truth, He empowers us to do so even in the midst of difficulty, by giving us a new heart and the Holy Spirit.

- Coach, what would you be teaching your athletes if you made rash promises to them to alleviate difficulty?
- What difficulty are you currently walking through as a coach that might tempt you to make rash promises to alleviate it? Ask the Lord to help you speak the truth instead, so He will be glorified as you are patient through your difficulty.

GAME CHANGER

Coach, know that as you face difficulty in all areas of your life, the Lord has not left you to your own strength to be patient through it. Instead, He has given you a new heart and the Holy Spirit to empower you to be patient in difficulty. He also understands what it means to be patient in difficulty as He in the person of Jesus, experienced incredible difficulty during His earthly ministry.

"[3] Consider him who endured from sinners such hostility against himself, so that you may not grow weary or fainthearted." – Hebrews 12:3

ONE BIG THING

What is the most significant lesson for you to take with you from this chapter?

IMPACT PRAYER

Father, in the midst of my difficulties enable me to be patient. Keep me from grumbling during difficulty or trying to alleviate it through rash promises. Remind me of those examples who have been patient in difficulty as well as Your purposes for me through my difficulties. In Jesus name I pray, Amen.

CHAPTER TWELVE
THE FAITH-FUELED COACH
PRAYER

JAMES 5:13-20

STUDY STARTER

As coaches, we have the great privilege and responsibility to coach, serve, lead, mentor and be an example to our athletes and other coaches. How are you serving, leading and being an example when it comes to prayer? In your own circumstances (suffering, good times, sickness) are you going to the Lord in prayer? Are you encouraging your athletes and fellow coaches to do the same? It is a great privilege to go to the Lord in prayer. Make it a point to embrace the privilege of prayer

STUDY PASSAGE

[13] Is anyone among you suffering? Let him pray. Is anyone cheerful? Let him sing praise. [14] Is anyone among you sick? Let him call for the elders of the church, and let them pray over him, anointing him with oil in the name of the Lord. [15] And the prayer of faith will save the one who is sick, and the Lord will raise him up. And if he has committed sins, he will be forgiven. [16] Therefore, confess your sins to one another and pray for one another, that you may be healed. The prayer of a righteous person has great power as it is working. [17] Elijah was a man with a nature like ours, and he prayed fervently that it might not rain, and for three years and six months it did not rain on the earth. [18] Then he prayed again, and heaven gave rain, and the earth bore its fruit. [19] My brothers, if anyone among you wanders from the truth and someone brings him back, [20] let him know that whoever brings back a sinner from his wandering will save his soul from death and will cover a multitude of sins.

STUDY HELP

- **v. 13 – "suffering"** = *hardship, calamity; enduring evil treatment by people.*
- **v. 14 – "sick"** = *without strength; feeble; weak. (It is used in the N.T. to refer to both physical sickness (18 times) and spiritual sickness (14 times).*
- **v. 14 – "elders"** = *spiritual shepherds in the local church.*
- **v. 15 – "save"** = *rescue; preserve; keep from harm.*
- **v. 16 – "confess"** = *to say the same thing; agree to call sin, sin.*
- **v. 16 – "healed"** = *renewed.*
- **v. 16 – "righteous"** = *to be made right with God through faith in Jesus.*
- **v. 19 – "brothers"** = *anyone, male or female, who is part of the family of God through faith in Jesus.*
- **v. 19 – "wanders"** = *strays; roam about; be deceived.*
- **v. 20 – "brings back"** = *turns around.*
- **v. 20 – "cover ... sins"** = *cause to be forgotten.*

EXTRA HELP

As we begin examining this passage of scripture, it is important that we see it in its proper context. The first 6 verses of chapter 5 dealt with persecution—the persecution of the godly by the ungodly rich. Then, in verses 7-12, James exhorted his readers and us to respond to this persecution by patiently enduring it. This is obviously easier said than done. God knows this, so He inspires James to write these verses (vv. 13-20) on prayer.

This pattern of persecution, patiently enduring and prayer is the exact same way James began this letter in chapter 1: verse 2 = persecution (trials), verses 3-4 = patiently endure, verses 5-8 = pray. This prescription is so important that James ends his letter with the same emphasis.

STUDY QUESTIONS

1. According to verses 13-15, in what circumstances does James call us to pray? What motivation does he give us to embrace this exhortation?

2. Based on verse 16, why is it important to confess our sins to one another? How could this practice build trust in your relationships?

3. In verse 15, what three results of prayer does James mention?

4. Verse 16 refers to a "righteous person." How would you define a "righteous person?"

5. According to verse 19, what are we called to do for those who wander from the truth?

6. Based on verse 20, what are the results of bringing back "a sinner from his wandering?"

STUDY SUMMARY

God desires you and your team to pray in all situations for the purpose of rescuing some and restoring others.

COACHING CONNECTION

Coach, our faith in Jesus fuels our ability to be coaches of prayer.

KEYS TO WINNING

▶ **VIDEO GUIDE AT KINGDOMSPORTS.ONLINE**

▶ **FOLLOW THE EXHORTATION TO PRAY**

In verses 13-16a James exhorts us to prayer in three main circumstances: in suffering, when you are cheerful and in sickness. These circumstances are familiar to all of us.

Look with me at the first circumstance in which we are exhorted to pray beginning with the first phrase in verse 13: "Is anyone among you suffering?" In light of the book of James this suffering most likely included: trials (1:2-4), temptations (1:13-18), prejudice (2:1-7), being injured by the tongue (3:1-12), being spoken against (4:11-12) and injustice (5:1-6). And notice in verse 13 what James calls one to do then—"Let him pray. In the midst of suffering, we are to continually come to the Lord in prayer seeking His comfort and grace.

Let's now look at the second circumstance in which we are exhorted to pray found in verse 13, "Is anyone cheerful?" When we find ourselves with an inner attitude of cheerfulness in spite of persecution or difficulty James calls us to "sing praise." Praising the Lord is to be an ongoing practice in the life of a follower of Jesus as we find cheerfulness in the midst of adversity. Singing praises to the Lord is an aspect of prayer.

The third circumstance in which the Lord through James exhorts us to pray is found in verse 14 with the phrase, "Is anyone among you sick?" The word "sick" means to be without strength or weak (physical or spiritual). The context of James as a whole, as well as the immediate context of chapter 5, is James addressing Christians who are undergoing mistreatment and persecution and are now sick (weak and weary). James instructs these believers to call on the elders of the church to pray for them so that they might be lifted up or renewed.

In verse 15, we see that God uses the prayers of the elders (verse 14) to deliver the weak and defeated believer from a state of spiritual weakness to a state of spiritual strength. The Lord uses believers to help lift up other followers of Jesus from spiritual weariness. And so James exhorts us to confess our sin to other followers of Jesus (verse 16a). Praying for each other helps in overcoming that sin and the weariness in our lives.

- Coach, when you are suffering what is your normal first response? How would the Lord call you to respond according to verse 13?

- Coach, what is your normal first response after a victory (time of cheerfulness)? How would the Lord call you to respond according to verse 13?

- Coach, make it a point to know when your athletes are weak and weary (physically or spiritually) so you can pray for them. What is your plan to do this?

_____
_____
_____
_____
_____
_____

▶ UNDERSTAND THE ILLUSTRATION OF PRAYER

James further encourages us to prayer by presenting an illustration. He begins with the following words in verse 16b, "The prayer of a righteous person has great power as it is working." If you are in Jesus through faith in His death, burial and resurrection to conquer sin, then you are a righteous person whose prayer "has great power as it is working."

In verses 17-18 James points to Elijah as an illustration of a righteous person whose prayer had great power as it was working. James tells how Elijah prayed that it would not rain and then after three and a half years he prayed it would rain again and it did (1 Kings 17-18). This was a familiar story to James' readers and is a great illustration of how the Lord uses prayer to accomplish his purposes.

Why would James use this illustration? Some of the believers who were not elders may have thought, "I am just an ordinary Christian, not an elder and certainly not Elijah. How can I pray for someone to be restored or hear their confession of sin?" Notice again the phrase in verse 17: "Elijah was a man with a nature like ours." James seeks to disarm the excuse that Elijah was some superhuman with whom his readers could not relate. Elijah proved himself to be like us when, after his prayer and subsequent defeat of the 450 prophets of Baal, he ran from Jezebel (Kings 19). James' point is that if Elijah can be effective in prayer for the glory of God, so can you.

- Coach, do you believe your prayer has great power to accomplish the Lord's will? Why or why not?

- Why can you trust that the Lord will use your prayer to accomplish His will?

- How can you practically encourage your athletes and other coaches to believe the Lord can use their prayers to accomplish His will?

_____
_____
_____
_____
_____

▶ BE AN ANSWER TO PRAYER

As evidenced from verses 13-18 the Lord uses prayer to accomplish his purposes, therefore it is important to pray. Not only is it important to pray, but it is also important to understand that the Lord often uses us to be an answer to prayer.

The context of verses 19-20 is that of a Christ-follower who is spiritually weak (sick) as a result of sin (not all weakness/sickness is a result of our personal sin). They fail to call the elders of the church to come to lift them up in prayer and they fail to confess their sin to another Christian for the purpose of being helped (vv. 14-16). The consequences of not dealing with sin can be devastating and destructive, so James gives instruction on how to be an answer to prayer by helping to restore them.

When a brother or sister in Christ "wanders from the truth" James calls us to be an answer to prayer by bringing them "back." James says in verse 20 when we restore a fellow believer in Christ from wandering it will "save his soul from death and will cover a multitude of sins." What does this mean? James points to two results of being an answer to prayer by restoring a wandering believer. First, based on the context of James 5, to "save his soul from death" is referring to a person being saved from physical danger or death. When a child of God departs from the truth and sins and then fails to deal with their sin, it will result in discipline from the Lord – which can even be physical death (i.e. Acts 5:5, 10; 1 Corinthians 11:29-32).

The second result of being an answer to prayer by restoring a wandering Christian is found in the last phrase of verse 20: "will cover a multitude of sins." When a wandering believer turns from their sin – they experience the forgiveness of sin that is already theirs in Christ. The person who has been restored is not to be treated as a 2nd class Christian but is rather to be received with open and gracious arms, because of the grace of God working in their lives.

- Coach, has anyone restored you in a state of wandering? How did that impact your life?
- Are there athletes or coaches in your program who are wandering? What is your plan to be an answer to prayer by graciously restoring them?

GAME CHANGER

Coach, know that Jesus understands what it is to walk through persecution and difficulty. Not only does He understand, but through faith in Him, He gives us the privilege to approach the Father in prayer. When we do approach Him in prayer, we find all the grace and mercy that we, and the others for whom we are praying, will need.

"15 For we do not have a high priest who is unable to sympathize with our weaknesses, but one who in every respect has been tempted as we are, yet without sin. 16 Let us then with confidence draw near to the throne of grace, that we may receive mercy and find grace to help in time of need." – Hebrews 4:15-16

ONE BIG THING

What is the most significant lesson for you to take with you from this chapter?

www.ingramcontent.com/pod-product-compliance
Lightning Source LLC
Chambersburg PA
CBHW072038110526
44592CB00012B/1464

IMPACT PRAYER

Father, I confess that my first response to suffering, or when I am cheerful, or when sick or weary is not always to come to You in prayer. By Your grace, empower me daily to make my first response to whatever I face be crying out to You in prayer. Also, empower me to be an answer to prayer by lovingly helping restore those who are being weighed down by sin and beginning to wander. In Jesus name I pray, Amen.

CONCLUSION

The title of this study is **The Faith-Fueled Coach: A Bible Study for Coaches Who want to Put Their Faith Into Action.** If you have completed all twelve chapters, you have been challenged to put your faith into action. Take this opportunity to write out a prayer to God that articulates your desire to be a coach who wants to put your faith into action and ask for His grace to help you do so.

_____
_____
_____
_____
_____